Curtains and Blinds

Contents

Before you Begin: Blinds   56

Making Blinds   64

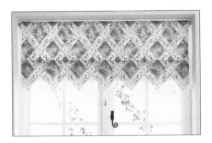

Sewing Techniques   74

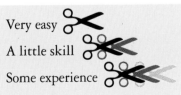

Very easy

A little skill

Some experience

First Decisions

In the same way that a room's colour scheme will affect the choice of fabric, the style, position and shape of a window will dictate the type of window treatment that will be most effective. However, there are still many other factors to consider.

This chapter provides ideas for window treatments for a range of window shapes and situations. It looks at the wide range of fabrics and linings available, giving information on their suitability for different types of curtain or blind, as well as providing details on the alternative hanging systems and the kits and accessories that are available.

This chapter contains

Choosing a style

There is a wide range of window shapes and styles, with no right way to dress any particular one. The room's use, its colour scheme and furnishing style, and the window's aspect are all factors that need to be considered when choosing a style of window treatment.

▲ Windows can often be improved with a grand treatment of floor draping curtains and a decorative top edge. A simple way to provide interest is to match up a length of fabric and wrap it around the pole. The apparent size can be increased by fixing the hanging system above or to the sides of the window.

◄ An alternative treatment for small windows is to make one window sized curtain held to the side with a tieback.

▲ Windows with an interesting view look best with a simple treatment that frames the outlook.

▲ Recessed windows can be treated in several ways. Hang floor length curtains outside the recess or fit curtains or blinds inside. A combination of both in complementary fabrics can also be used for stronger impact.

▲ Kitchens and bathrooms need treatments that are easy to clean and care for. Roller or Roman blinds keep fabric out of the way of work areas and surfaces. If daytime privacy is required consider a half-window café curtain or flat panel tied to a rod.

▲ Bay windows often look best with a simple treatment that shows off the decorative shape. Roman blinds made to cover each window independently can be used to act as sun shades when necessary. Add curtains outside the bay for a more lavish effect.

▲ Windows without a view can be successfully screened with sheer blinds. Consider festoon or Roman blinds in a translucent fabric. One large curtain fixed across the top edge and partially draped to one side is another decorative alternative.

Choosing fabrics

When buying fabric for curtains consider the weight of the fabric and how it drapes, its resistance to fading and soiling, and the ease with which it can be cleaned.

TYPES OF FIBRE

Fabrics may be produced from natural or man-made fibres, or a mixture of the two. Natural fibres, which include cotton, linen, silk and wool, are resistant to dust and dirt and clean well, though some can fade and shrink when washed. Pure linen and silk fabrics crease easily.

Man-made fibres can be totally synthetic like polyester, nylon and acrylic, or derived from plant material, which is then chemically treated, like viscose. Man-made fibres are usually easy to wash, are crease- and shrink-resistant and tough. However they attract dust and dirt, so need more regular cleaning than natural fibres. Man-made fibres are often mixed with natural fibres so that the fabric contains the benefits of each.

SHEER FABRICS

Lace

Lace can be made from cotton, man-made fibres or a mixture of the two. The ornamental open-work patterns make it ideal for use as a decorative screen.

Muslin

This is a fine, open-weave cotton that is available in white or cream and drapes well. Its translucence makes it ideal for full, sheer curtains.

Voile

Voile can be pure cotton, polyester or a polyester-cotton mix and is available in plain colours and printed motifs. It is ideal for festoon blinds as well as curtains.

Synthetic sheers

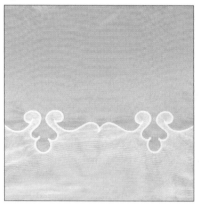

Sheer fabrics made from synthetic fibres are tough and easily washed. A wide range of widths are available and, some sheers come with decorative edging and a casing.

CURTAIN FABRICS
Printed cotton

Most cottons are hard-wearing and drape well. Lightweight polyester-cotton mixes, which are strong and fade resistant, are suitable for smaller lined curtains and blinds.

Calico

A cheap, firm, unbleached cotton; calico drapes well but is prone to shrinkage and creasing. It is most effective for lavish window treatments.

Woven cotton

Medium-weight tightly woven cotton is best for blinds but for roller blinds the fabric must be stiffened first.

Gingham

This lightweight cotton or polyester-cotton fabric comes with a woven check. An attractive, simple fabric ideal for kitchens and bathrooms.

Linen union

Made from a blend of cotton and linen, often with some added nylon, linen union is hard wearing and firm but needs careful washing and can fade.

Velvet

A deep-pile fabric made from silk, cotton or synthetic fibres. The pile must always run in the same direction. Velvet requires care.

Linings, kits and accessories

Lining curtains protects the main curtain fabric and improves the way the curtains hang. Lining fabrics tend to wear out before the main fabric, so invest in the best quality you can afford.

Including an interlining, an extra layer of material designed to be sandwiched between the main fabric and the lining, adds insulation, thickness and weight.

A variety of kits are available that make window treatments quicker and easier to produce. There is also a range of specialist accessories that add a professional touch to the finished effect.

LINING FABRIC

Cotton sateen

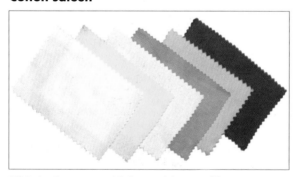

This is the most widely used lining fabric. It comes in a standard 120cm (48in) width and a wider 137cm (54in) width, plus a wide range of colours. Easycare polyester cotton fabrics in plain colours are also suitable, as is wide-width cotton poplin.

Blackout lining

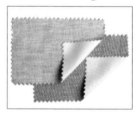

This polyester cotton lining is designed to exclude the light and comes in shades of grey, white or ecru (natural).

Thermal lining

There are two types of thermal lining. A cotton/acrylic mix that comes in white or ecru (natural), and a more expensive alternative with an aluminium coating.

INTERLININGS

Interlinings are available in a wide range of thicknesses and fibres, in two widths 120cm (48in) and 137cm (54in), and in white and ecru. Used to add body and insulation to curtains the usual choices are *bump*: for medium to heavyweight curtains, *ribbed interlining*: a mixed fibre alternative, *raised interlining*: allergy-free and made from man-made fibres and *domette*: a smoother interlining, most suited to lightweight printed cottons.

KITS

Blind kits

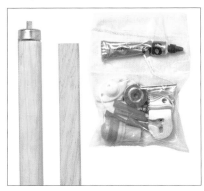

Kits for making blinds are available in a range of sizes. They contain all you need to make up a blind with your own fabric and usually include appropriate wall fixings.

Eyelet kits

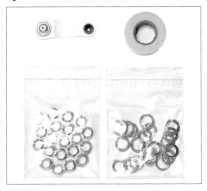

These kits allow you to produce interlaced and tied headings easily. You can also buy packs of eyelets and a tool from most haberdashery departments.

Tab-top kits

The kit includes iron-on buckram strips, plus button shapes for covering with your own fabric and pins and butterfly clips to fix. No sewing is necessary.

ACCESSORIES

Pelmet former

A PVC sheet with adhesive on both sides (or one adhesive side with a felt backing), with pelmet shapes pre-printed on the backing paper.

Cord tidy

This is designed to hold heading cords neatly after they have been pulled up to gather curtains or blinds.

Grip Tape (Velcro)

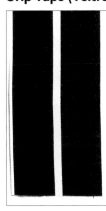

A simple way to attach lightweight fixed curtains, Roman blinds, valances and bed coronets; allowing easy removal for cleaning.

Leadweight tape

Stitched into curtain hems, leadweights help the curtains to hang well. Available in light, medium and heavyweight lengths or as button-shaped weights.

Curtain clips

Available in a wide range of styles, clips can be used to hang fixed lightweight curtains, blinds and valances.

Tracks, poles and rods

Hanging systems for window treatments fall into two main categories, those that are hidden behind the treatment and those that form a decorative part of the overall effect.

Tracks, which are usually cheaper than poles, fall into the first category. They can be shaped to go round a curve in a bay window or fit neatly into a recess.

Wooden, brass or iron poles form an integral part of the finished effect. Although some types of pole can be mitred or bent, they are best suited to straight runs.

CURTAIN TRACK

Curtain tracks are suitable for light to medium-weight curtains, are usually plastic and come in a wide range of lengths, with fixing brackets, slip-on hooks for hanging the curtain, and end-stops to hold the hooks on the track.

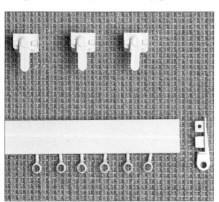

Some tracks have curtain hooks with rings below to take curtains with detachable linings. Other alternatives include expandable steel track and track systems with integral cording, allowing the curtains to be drawn from one side.

VALANCE RAIL

Valance rails are available as a single rail to take a valance on its own or as a combined track and rail, where curtains hang from the track behind and the valance hooks over the rail in front.

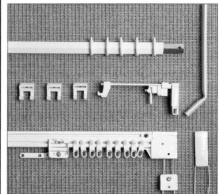

BLIND TRACK

This is designed for use with Austrian or festoon blinds. Apart from the curtain track with curtain hooks and cord tidies to take the blind's pulled-up vertical cords, it has cord holders which slide into position above each length of vertical tape to take the pulley cords and a cord lock at one end.

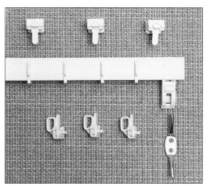

WOODEN POLES

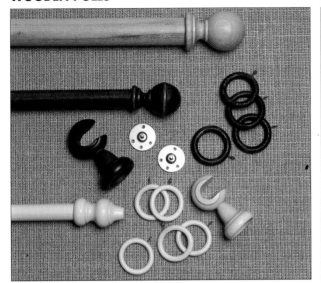

Poles are available in a range of thicknesses, in natural or dark stained finishes or painted in colours. With some kits, matching end finials, rings and wall brackets for fixing are supplied, with others they come separately.

BRASS POLES

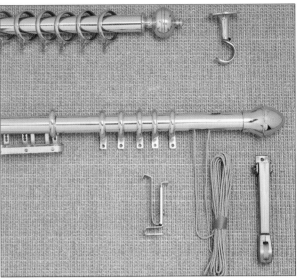

Brass, or brass-finished poles, come in a wide range of thicknesses and in some cases are expandable. In other instances the front view of the pole hides runners for hanging the curtains and an integral cording set.

IRON POLES

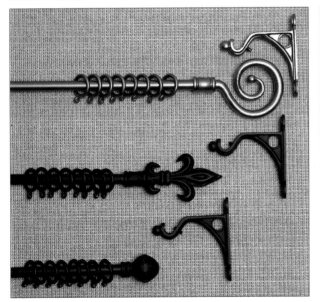

These are slim and strong. Some have simple curved ends others have very decorative finials and come with fixing brackets and rings. Plain iron rods can be used to take cut out and tab or tied on curtains without the use of rings.

STRETCH WIRES AND PLASTIC COATED RODS

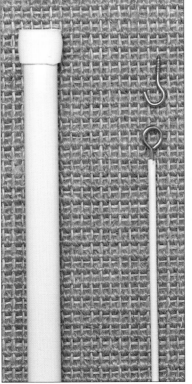

This type of hanging system is usually used for sheer or café curtains where the curtain remains across the window. The wire or rod slips through a channel in the top of the curtain and is then attached to the frame with hooks. A rod may be telescopic, designed to grip the inside wall of the recess, or have end sockets that screw into the walls.

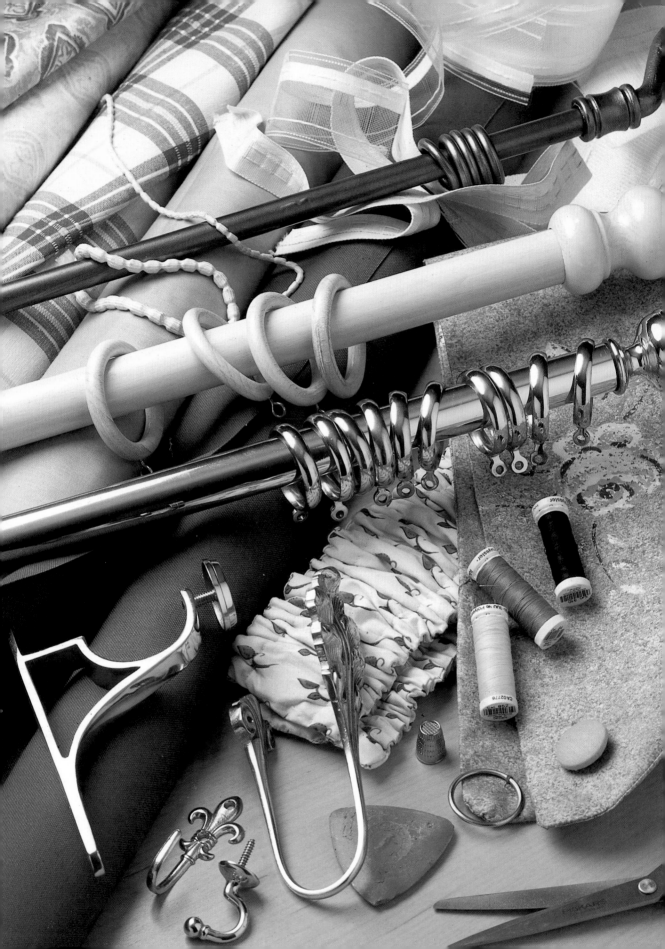

Before you Begin: Curtains

Once the style of curtain treatment has been chosen and the type of hanging system decided upon, fabric can be bought and work on making up can get underway.

This chapter explains clearly how to fix the hanging system in place, measure the window and then calculate the amount of fabric that will be required. With tips on what to look for when buying fabric, information on how to calculate fabric quantities for different types of heading tape and, most importantly, how to cut out and join fabric so that patterns match, it provides a framework for achieving professional looking results.

Curtain style, size and shape

When choosing a window treatment, consider not only the overall style that you want to create, but practicalities such as curtain length. Curtains are usually made to one of four lengths depending on the window style, shape and position.

◀ A large window in a large room can take a more elaborate treatment that includes a decorative topping of valance, pelmet or swags and tails. In a small room bold fabric patterns and lavish treatments can be overpowering, so keep to fabrics that blend with the surrounding decorations and add interest with complementary borders, cords or fringes.

FLOOR DRAPED CURTAINS
Extra long curtains that drape over the floor are now very popular. Usually a drape of about 30cm (12in) is adequate.

◀ To make a small window appear larger, fix the hanging system above or to the sides of the window.

▲ Sheer curtains can be light, airy and simple or sumptuously gathered, crossed and tied back. Also consider lace roller blinds or organdie or muslin festoon or roman blinds.

▲ To create the illusion of width on tall, narrow windows, use a pelmet or valance in a complementary fabric and match this up with a wide border at the base.

FLOOR LENGTH CURTAINS

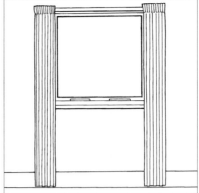

Measure from the track to the floor and deduct 1.25cm (½in) so that the curtains sit just above the floor, reducing wear along the hem edge.

ABOVE A RADIATOR

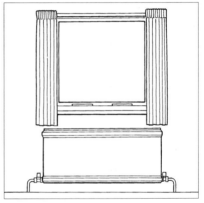

Where a radiator is placed immediately below a window make short curtains to avoid holding back the heat. Measure to the radiator top, then deduct 1.25cm (½in) for a sensible curtain length.

RECESSED WINDOW

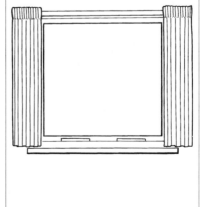

A window in a recess with a wide sill requires curtains to sill level. Measure from the track, pole or rail to the sill and deduct 1.25cm (½in) for finished curtain length. For curtains hung outside the recess, measure to a wide sill or, if narrow, add between 5-10cm (2-5in) for the curtain to hang just below the sill.

Heading styles

A wide range of ready-made tapes are available for use on both curtains and valances as well as for gathered blinds. Your choice of heading will affect the quantity of fabric you need, the way the fabric drapes and the overall effect of the curtain.

Most wider tapes can be used so that the heading hides the track or alternatively the curtains can be hung from rings on a pole.

PENCIL PLEAT

The tape for pencil pleats is stiff and when pulled up forms slim, straight pleats that are close together. Narrower widths are most suited to shorter curtains or valances, while the widest width suits full length curtains.

Widths available: 3.9cm (1½in), 7.3cm (3in), 13.8cm (5½in) plus for nets and sheer fabrics a translucent tape 6cm (2½in).

Fabric requirement: two-and-a-half times track, pole or rod length.

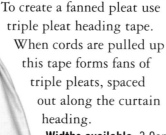

TRIPLE-PLEAT

To create a fanned pleat use triple pleat heading tape. When cords are pulled up this tape forms fans of triple pleats, spaced out along the curtain heading.

Widths available: 3.9cm (1½in), 8.5cm (3¼in), 13.8cm (5½in).

Fabric requirement: twice the track, pole or rod length.

GATHERED HEADING

This tape is narrower and usually placed slightly below the top edge of the curtain. It is available either as a traditional gathered heading or to form clustered gathers. This is often used where the heading will be covered by a pelmet or valance. Special tape for nets and sheers is also available.

Widths available: 2.5cm (1in) standard tape, 1.7cm (⅜in) net tape.

Fabric requirement: one-and-a-half to two times track, pole or rod length.

LINING TAPE

This is designed for use with detachable linings. It has an opening along the lower edge which the raw top edge of the curtain lining slips into. The stitching then traps the lining inside. The tape is gathered to fit the curtains and the hooks added.

BOX PLEATS

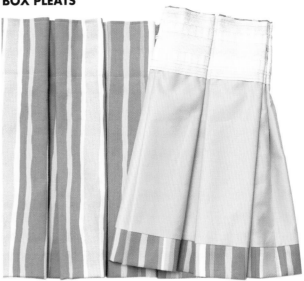

The tape forms closely spaced box pleats. This type of heading is designed to be a decorative finish on a valance or curtains which remains in a fixed position.
Width available: 8cm (3in)
Fabric requirement: three times track length.

SMOCKED FINISH

A smocked heading forms a decorative finish for valances and curtains, and is also ideal for fine nets and sheers. When the tape is pulled up it creates an effect like smocking.
Width available: 8cm (3in).
Fabric requirement: two-and-a-half times track, pole or rod length.

GOBLET PLEATS

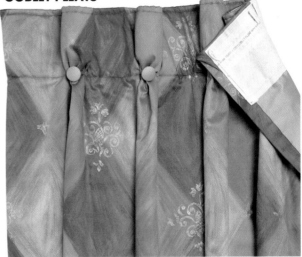

Until recently goblet pleats had to be constructed by hand. A tape is now available that produces these grand goblet-shaped pleats with three smaller pleats falling from the stem point.
Width available: 13.8cm (5½in).
Fabric requirement: two-and-a-quarter times track or pole length.

Fixing curtain tracks and poles

Both curtain tracks and poles are fixed in place with brackets. In most cases these come as part of the kit together with fixing screws.

How you fix the track or pole depends on where you decide to place it. They may be fixed to a timber window frame or to a masonry or stud wall. All require different methods of fixing.

FIXING SCREWS

Timber

When screwing into timber, start by marking the position for the screw with a bradawl. To make it easier to fix the screw drill a short hole, slightly smaller than the screw size, before driving the screw home with a screwdriver.

Masonry walls

When fixing a screw into a solid masonry wall you will first need to fit a wall plug into the hole. Use a masonry bit to drill the hole. Drill bit, screw and wall plug should all match in size. Make a starting hole by turning the drill by hand, then drill the hole to the length of the wall plug. Insert the plug and drive the screw home with a screwdriver.

Cavity walls

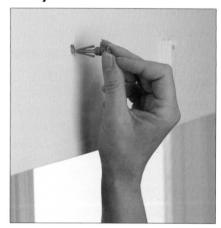

Partition walls are often made of plasterboard attached to timber struts (studs) with a cavity behind the plasterboard. To fix a screw into the studs you can use the same method as for timber.

When fixing a screw into the cavity use a special wallplug with a toggle that opens to form an anchor against the back of the plasterboard as the screw is tightened. Drill a hole to fit the wallplug, push it though and drive the screw home. This type of fixing is only suitable for lightweight curtains.

CURTAIN TRACKS

Most curtain tracks can be fixed into the ceiling or into the wall. If you want to fix the track into the ceiling to ensure that the fixing can take the weight, screw the brackets into a joist. When fixing the track just above a window that has a concrete lintel above it you will probably need to fix the track to a batten. In this case ensure that the batten is longer than the lintel so that you can drill into the wall beyond it.

Once the batten is fixed, it can be painted or papered to make it less obvious and the track brackets can then be screwed to it.

CURTAIN POLES

Curtain pole brackets are fixed in much the same way as track brackets. The two brackets that come with a pole are designed to be fixed about 8-10cm (3-5in) in from the pole end with one ring placed in the space left at each end.

1 To position the brackets, first draw a line along the wall where the track is to be fixed. Use a spirit level to make sure that the line is horizontal. Check the manufacturer's guidelines for spacing the brackets, then mark the position for each bracket along the line, placing the first and last brackets about 5cm (2in) in from the ends of the track.

2 Once all the brackets are fixed, attach the track to them, slide on the gliders, and position the end stops. With some tracks the hooks are first attached to the curtain and then slotted into the gliders, with others the hooks and gliders are combined and the curtain heading is slipped over these.

Buying curtain fabric

Before buying fabric it is essential to work out precisely the amount of fabric that you require, taking into consideration the hanging system and the heading tape to be used, and most importantly the size of pattern repeat on your chosen fabric. Most fabrics carry labels that give information on fibres and recommended uses as well as cleaning instructions.

BUYING TIPS

- **Colour matching:** Take samples; a colour chart, carpet off-cut and fabric swatches with you to check colour compatibility.
- **Colour checks:** Take home a small sample or pattern repeat of the chosen fabric to check the effect of the fabric in both day and artificial light.
- **Crease resistance:** Crease up a corner of fabric in your hand to check whether the fabric remains crumpled.
- **Shrinkage:** If you intend to wash your curtains buy pre-shrunk fabric or check with the supplier for shrinkage, then buy extra fabric accordingly.
- **Pattern repeat:** Check the length of the pattern repeat and add this to each curtain length when calculating the amount of fabric required.
- **Fabric flaws:** Before the fabric is cut, check the length carefully for flaws and make sure the pattern has been printed straight and follows the fabric grain.
- **Safety and wear:** Use flame and stain-resistant fabrics for children's rooms. These finishes can be applied as a spray after making up.

PATTERN REPEAT

If you choose a fabric with a design that needs to be matched across the width you will need to allow extra fabric. Suppliers will usually check the pattern repeat and help you to calculate the amount of extra fabric that you will need. A bold motif looks best if the bottom of the design sits on the lower hem edge, so allow for this too. Pelmets and valances in the same fabric as the curtain or blind look better when pattern matched.

MEASURING UP AND CALCULATING FABRIC QUANTITIES

Before you can calculate the fabric you require, decide on the track or pole and the heading tape you need to achieve the desired finished effect. Follow the simple procedure below to work out your fabric requirements.

CALCULATING HEADING TAPE

Measurement W (see step 3 below) gives you the length of heading tape you will need. Add 10cm-20cm (4-8in) to allow for pleat positions and pulling cord ends out.

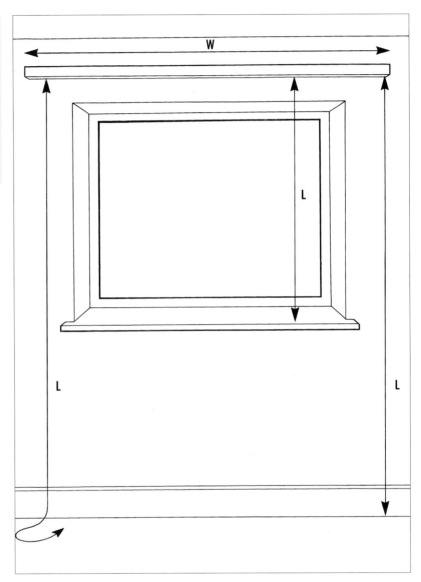

1 Choose your track or pole (see pages 12-13), decide on the position and then measure the length that you require. Fix the track or pole in place (see pages 20-21) to ensure accurate measurement of the finished fabric length.

2 Decide on the curtain length (see pages 16-17) and measure this from the track or pole. Add 8cm (3in) for the heading (more for a deep heading tape) and 15cm (6in) for hem allowance. Call this measurement L.

3 Select a heading style (see pages 18-19) and check the fabric fullness required – usually between one-and-a-half and three times the track length. Measure the length of the track or pole and multiply this length by the fabric fullness, adding 25cm (10in) for side hems. If the track overlaps at the centre add a further 30cm (12in). Call this measurement W.

4 To calculate the number of fabric widths required, divide measurement W into the width of the chosen fabric. Where the measurement lies between two widths round up to the next full width.

5 Multiply the number of widths required by the length L to find the amount of fabric required.

Cutting out and pattern matching

Take care when cutting out fabric as a mistake could prove to be expensive. It is worth stopping and double checking your calculations and measurements before using the scissors. Once the first two lengths of fabric have been cut these are used as a pattern for all the following lengths needed to make up the curtain width.

WORK AREA

If possible set up a separate working area so that you do not have to tidy away the materials every time you stop working. Alternatively, use the largest open area in the house.

Sewing machine: place the machine on a solid surface, well lit by natural light. A working light is a useful addition.

Iron and ironing board: leave these set up and ready for use at any time during sewing. Regular pressing ensures a professional finish.

Work table: use a large, rectangular table for cutting out and for laying out lengths of fabric prior to pinning, tacking or stitching. Alternatively, use the largest floor area covered with a sheet of plastic or old sheeting.

PREPARING FABRIC

Before cutting out, press the fabric and ensure that the top edge, cut in the shop, is straight with the grain of the fabric. To do this, lay the fabric out on a flat surface and place a set square, or other square cornered object, on the top edge to get a right angle. Extend the top edge of the right angle with a metre or yard rule and draw a line alongside it with tailor's chalk. Cut along the top edge following the drawn line and remove selvages down either side.

PLAIN FABRIC

Carefully measure out the first length and make a mark with tailor's chalk on each side edge of the fabric. Join up the marks and then cut out. Use this length as a template for cutting out the other lengths required to make up each curtain.

PATTERNED FABRIC

Careful planning is needed before cutting out patterned fabrics. On curtains (and festoon or Austrian blinds) the lower edge of the design should sit on the finished lower hem edge. The pattern should match up vertically with the curtains on a valance heading.

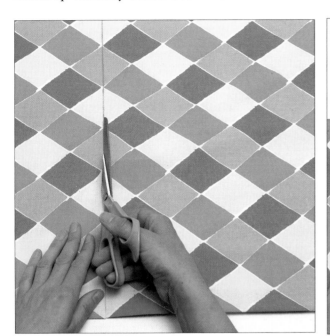

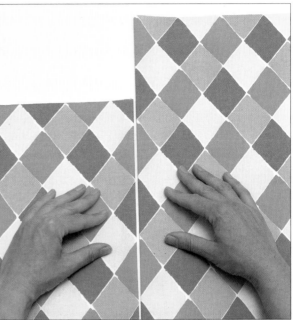

1 Carefully measure out the first length, making sure that the pattern is correctly positioned and allowing for hem turnings below the lower pattern edge, then make a mark with tailor's chalk on each side edge of the fabric. Join up the marks and cut out.

2 To match the pattern across widths, place the cut length on a flat surface and position the uncut fabric beside it. Move the cut length up and down until the pattern matches exactly with that on the uncut fabric, then mark up and cut out the next length. Repeat using this method to cut out all the lengths required.

JOINING LENGTHS

If it is necessary to attach any half widths to make up the required width of fabric for a curtain or blind, position these on the outer side of each curtain where they will be less noticeable.

Simply pin a length of fabric in half down the length and cut along the fold. Attach these half widths down the outer side of each curtain, matching any motifs carefully on patterned fabrics.

Making Curtains

Your choice of curtain will depend not only on the overall style that you wish to create but also on the room where the curtains are to be used and the function that they are to perform. Unlined curtains, for example, are ideal for kitchens and bathrooms as they are easy to wash. Sheer and café curtains, which provide privacy whilst still allowing sunlight into a room, are a good choice for rooms that are overlooked or have an unattractive view.

Once decisions about the style of curtain and the hanging system have been made, it is possible to start making up. This chapter contains the techniques for making a variety of the most popular types of curtain, from simple unlined curtains to more complex interlined curtains.

Unlined curtains

Unlined curtains are easy to make and are a practical choice for kitchens, bathrooms or a child's playroom, especially if they are made from an easycare washable fabric like a mixture of polyester and cotton.

Each curtain is formed from single or joined widths of fabric, with hems at side and lower edges and heading tape along the top. If part widths are needed to make up the curtain size, attach these at the outer edge of each curtain.

MATERIALS: Light to medium-weight furnishing fabric, matching thread, pencil pleat heading tape, track or pole

FABRIC: To calculate the amount of fabric required, follow the instructions for measuring the window and calculating fabric quantities (see pages 22-23). You will need a length of curtain tape the width of each finished curtain, plus 10cm (4in) to allow for positioning.

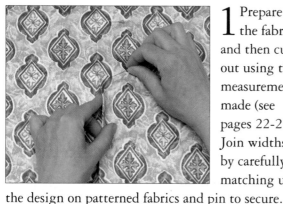

1 Prepare the fabric and then cut out using the measurements made (see pages 22-23). Join widths by carefully matching up the design on patterned fabrics and pin to secure.

2 Tack pinned widths together. Work plain fabric from the back. On patterned fabric work from the right side and use ladder stitch (see pages 78-79) to ensure that the design matches exactly. Stitch widths together using flat fell seams (see pages 80-81).

3 Turn under a 1.25cm (½in) hem to the wrong side on the side edges and press, then fold again to form a 3.5cm (1½in) double hem. Press and tack. Close to the inside edge of each hem, machine or slipstitch hem in place (see pages 80-81).

4 Turn down the top edge of the fabric to the width of the heading tape and press. Position the top edge of the tape 5mm (¼in) down from the folded top edge and covering the fabric raw edge. Allow a 5cm (2in) tape overlap at each end. Pin tape in position and tack to secure.

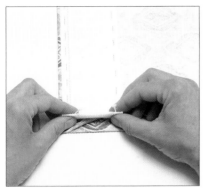

5 To neaten tape ends trim any excess tape, turn under a 5cm (2in) overlap and tack in place. On the edge where the curtain meets, knot the cords first and include in the overlap but, on the outside edge, pull the cords to the front of the tape ready for gathering up.

6 Stitch the tape in place, first along the top and bottom edges, sewing in the same direction each time, then across the ends. Make sure that the stitching goes through the cords on the leading edge to fix them in position but do not catch the cords at the outer edge.

7 Before you stitch the hem, first check the curtain length. Pull up the cords in the heading tape and hang the curtains. Mark the position for the hem, remove the curtains, then press in and tack a double hem. For a neat finish, mitre the corners (see pages 82-83). Lastly, stitch the hem.

Detachable linings

Linings protect curtain fabric from the wear and tear caused by bright light and extremes of temperature, help to exclude the light and also provide some extra insulation.

Detachable linings attach to the back of the curtains and have several advantages over a fixed lining. Linings often wear more quickly than the main curtain fabric and need to be replaced. Detachable linings by their nature are easy to remove and replace and because they are not an integral part of the curtain, slight shrinkage will not create a problem in fit.

MATERIALS: Lining fabric (see pages 10-11), matching thread, slip-over lining heading tape

FABRIC: Follow the instructions for measuring the window and estimate quantities of fabric as for curtains, allowing for each curtain a lining width of one-and-a-half to twice the track length (see pages 22-23). Allow for a hem that lies 2cm (¾in) above the curtain hem edge. Calculate the amount of heading tape that you will need (see pages 22-23), allowing extra for positioning.

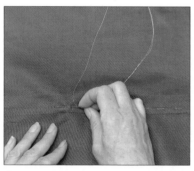

1 Cut out the lining fabric using the measurements you have made but allow for each finished lining to be 2.5cm (1in) narrower than the finished curtain. With right sides facing, tack and then stitch widths together using flat fell seams to enclose the raw edges (see pages 80-81).

2 To make the side hems, turn under a double 1.25cm (½in) hem and press. Machine stitch close to the inside edge of each hem.

3 Slip the heading tape over the raw top edge of the fabric, with the narrower side of the tape to the fabric right side. Pin in position, and trim tape to allow a 2.5cm (1in) overlap at each end. At the leading edge (where the curtains will meet), turn under a double 1.25cm (½in) hem to the wrong side. At the outside edge, pull the cords to the top side of the tape ready for gathering, then turn under a double 1.25cm (½in) in hem to the wrong side. Stitch across the tape ends, stitching through the cords on the leading edge to secure but leaving those at the outer edge free. Finally, stitch the tape to the curtain top edge.

4 Before you stitch the hem, check the lining length against the curtain. Place the curtain flat and then position the lining over the top of the curtain, matching top edge to hook positions. Turn up the hem 2cm (¾in) shorter than the curtain and stitch. Pull up the cords in the heading tape so that the lining is slightly narrower than the curtain. To hang a detachable lining, fix the hooks through the lining heading tape first, then through the curtain heading tape. Alternatively, hang the lining from separate rings positioned on some tracks below the heading tape hooks.

A LINING THAT SHOWS

If the lining peeps around the curtain in any position, spoiling the effect, cut short lengths of narrow tape and attach one half of a press fastener to the end. Stitch the opposite end to the inner side hem of the lining and stitch the corresponding fastener section to the inside side hem of the curtain. Fix fasteners.

Sheer curtains

Sheer curtains serve a practical purpose providing privacy for overlooked windows or hiding an unattractive view, but they can also be used for a purely decorative effect.

The curtain shown is designed to hang from a pole or track but sheers can also be made with a cased heading and hung from a curtain wire or rod.

When making sheer curtains, use wide width material avoiding seams as these show up as dark lines, and make hems as narrow as possible. Ensure that the fabric is cut square, as uneven raw edges will show on the right side. Use a set square or the table ends to check that the edges are straight before beginning.

MATERIALS: Sheer fabric, matching fine threads, covered wire/rail or rod/track, sheer heading tape if using a track

FABRIC: To calculate the amount of fabric required, follow the instructions for measuring the window and calculating fabric quantities (see pages 22-23). Add 20cm (8in) to the length to allow for hems and the heading tape, as well as 2cm (¾in) to the width for each side hem. If making a curtain to be hung from a lightweight track, you will need a length of tape the width of the finished curtain plus 10cm (4in).

CASED HEADING

1 Check that the fabric edge is square, then cut the number of fabric lengths required to make up the full size curtain. If you are using a patterned fabric, match the design and tack widths together using ladder stitch (see pages 78-79).

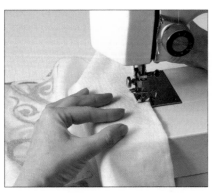

2 Join widths using narrow French seams (see pages 80-81). First stitch on the right side, 1cm (⅜in) outside the finished seamline position. Trim the raw edges to neaten them and, with right sides together, encase these raw edges in a second seam stitched 1cm (⅜in) from the first one.

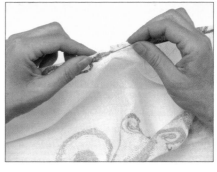

3 For side hems, turn in a double 1cm (⅜in) hem down each side edge and handstitch in place.

4 For the lower hem, turn up a double 2cm (¾in) hem and handstitch this.

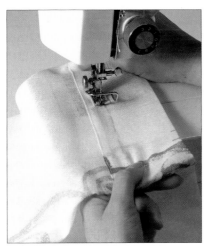

5 To finish the top edge with a casing for a wire or rod, fold over a single, narrow hem along the top edge of the curtain and tack. Fold over again to the frill and rod depth plus 5mm (¼in). Tack in place and machine stitch close to hem edge. Measure the casing depth from the stitched hem edge and draw a line across the fabric with tailor's chalk at this depth to divide the frill from the casing. Tack then stitch along marked line. Slot the wire or rod through the casing and hang the curtain.

APPLYING HEADING TAPE

To make a sheer curtain hung from a lightweight track, turn down a single 2.5cm (1in) hem along the top edge. Cut the heading tape to the width of the curtain plus 5cm (2in) overlap at each end. Position the top tape edge 3mm (⅛in) from the top hem edge and covering the fabric raw edge. Pin and tack in place. On the leading edge, pull the cords to the back of the tape, knot to secure and then turn in the tape overlap at each end and stitch in place (see step 6, pages 28-29). Pull up the gathering cords until the curtain is the correct width, even out the gathers, and hang the curtain.

Café curtains

Café curtains screen the lower section of a window while allowing light to pass through the top section. They can be made with a tabbed heading like the one shown here, a scalloped heading (see pages 40-41) or with a frilled heading and a casing through which to pass a stretch wire, pole or rod (see pages 32-33).

Small designs or plain colour fabrics are usually best for curtains with a short drop. Apart from cotton and polyester-cotton mixes, lighter semi-transparent fabrics like lace, net or voile are also suitable. On fine fabrics, line the facing with an interfacing to provide added strength to the fabric.

MATERIALS: Medium-weight furnishing or sheer fabric, matching thread, pole or rod

FABRIC: Fix the hanging system in place and measure from the underside to the sill, then add 5cm (2in). To work out the curtain width, measure the window from side to side and add half again or double the measurement. To calculate the amount of fabric required, divide the fabric width into the curtain width measurement, then multiply the number of widths by the curtain length. Allow extra for pattern match. You will also need enough fabric to make a curtain-wide facing 10cm (4in) in depth. For each tab you will also need a strip of fabric 20cm (8in) long by double the chosen tab width plus 2.5cm (1in).

1 Cut out the fabric lengths required to make up the curtain width and stitch together with flat fell seams (see pages 80-81). Carefully match the pattern on joined widths.

2 To make the side hems, turn in a double 1.25cm (½in) hem down each side edge, tack to secure and machine stitch down close to the hem edge.

3 Stitch together the widths of fabric for the facing with flat fell seams (see pages 80-81). Turn under a double 1.25cm (½in) hem on one long edge and machine stitch. Then on the right side of the curtain top edge, mark the tab positions with a fabric pencil. Either position tabs following the design of the fabric or space them out equally along the curtain width. Make sure that there is a tab at each end of the curtain.

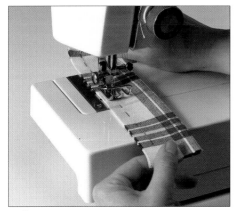

4 Cut strips of fabric for each tab 20cm (8in) long, making each piece twice the required tab width plus 2.5cm (1in). Fold each tab in half lengthways with right sides together, tack to secure and then stitch 1.25cm (½in) from the long raw edge. Press the seam open and turn the tab to the right side. Centre the seam and press well.

TAB KITS

Tab kits, which contain iron-on buckram cut to size, require no sewing. Simply follow the instructions provided to attach the buckram to your chosen tab fabric. The kits also contain self-cover buttons and butterfly clips to fix the heading in place.

5 Fold each tab in half across the width with the seam on the inside. Then, with raw ends matching up with the curtain top raw edge, line the tabs up with the pencil marks and pin in position on the right side of the fabric. Place the facing, wrong side uppermost, over the tab ends and curtain fabric, lining up raw edges. Pin and tack all three layers together across the top, stitch 1.25cm (½in) from the raw edge and then press.

6 Turn the curtain right side out, turn in the facing side hems and slipstitch to curtain sides. Before stitching the hem, hang the curtain and pin up the hem. Stitch, press and refix the curtain.

Lined curtains

Lined curtains hang better than unlined curtains and the lining helps to reduce the light, provides some insulation and protects the top fabric from sunlight damage.

The simplest way to make lined curtains, and the method used in this project, is to stitch the lining and top fabric together along the side and top edges and then take up the hems separately. The lining piece is cut narrower than the curtain width, so that when the curtain is turned right side out, the seams joining the two pieces are hidden at the back of the curtain.

MATERIALS: Furnishing fabric, lining fabric, matching sewing threads, deep triple pleat heading tape, track or pole

FABRIC: To calculate the amount of curtain fabric required, follow the instructions for measuring the window and calculating fabric quantities (see pages 22-23). You will need lining fabric to the finished curtain size. Use measurement W (see pages 22-23) to work out the amount of heading tape you require.

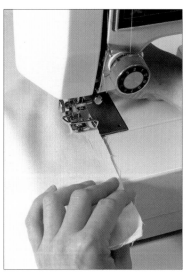

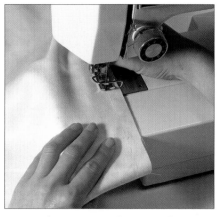

1 Cut the required lengths of fabric, allowing for pattern repeat, then pin and tack the widths together. On patterned fabric work from the right side using ladder stitch (see pages 78-79). Turn to the wrong side and stitch widths together with open seams 1.25cm (½in) from raw edge (see pages 80-81).

2 Cut lengths of lining 8cm (3in) shorter than the fabric length. With right sides facing, pin and then tack lining widths together, making a lining the width of the finished curtain. Stitch widths together with open seams. Then trim 5cm (2in) off each side edge of the lining.

3 Mark the top and lower edge centre points on fabric and lining. With right sides together, pin the lining to the curtain along one side edge. Offset the lining top edge from the fabric top edge by the width of the curtain tape; the centre point marks will not align at this point. Tack and stitch the side edge 1.25cm (½in) from the raw edge. Leave 10cm (4in) at the lower end unstitched. Do the same with the opposite side. The fabric, will be wider than the lining.

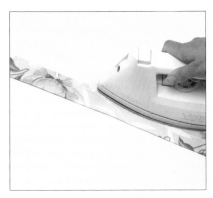

4 Turn the curtain to the right side and match up the centre points on the lining and fabric. Tack fabrics together along the lining top edge and pin together the bottom edges. Press well to form the curtain side edges and then remove pins. As the lining is narrower than the curtain fabric, there will be a 5cm (2in) overlap of the curtain fabric either side of the lining.

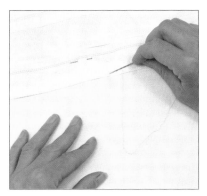

5 Fold over the fabric top edge to the wrong side so that it just covers the lining raw edge and pin in position. Position the tape just below the top edge, covering the fabric raw edge. Allow a 5cm (2in) overlap of tape at each end. Position tape pleats to allow for a flat area where curtains meet on one curtain, a pleat on the other, so that pleats appear at equal spaces across the curtains when they are drawn together. Tack in position and then stitch (see step 5 and 6, pages 28-29).

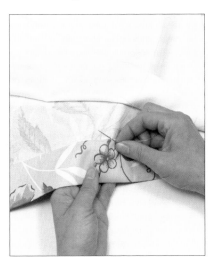

6 Before hemming the curtain, pull up the cords and hang the curtains to check the length. Pin up double hems on both the top fabric and lining fabric hem. The finished edge of the lining hem should lie 4cm (1⅜in) above the curtain hem and the finished curtain hem should be 5cm (2in) wide. Trim fabrics if necessary, mitre corners (see pages 82-83) and stitch lining and top fabric hems separately.

Interlined curtains

Interlined curtains have a thick layer of wadding sandwiched between the main fabric and the lining which adds extra insulation and provides a sumptuous look and feel to the curtains.

The main fabric and interlining are first lockstitched together to act as one layer and then the lining is lockstitched to this. Leadweight tape is included in the hem to ensure the curtains hang beautifully and a deep goblet heading completes the rich effect.

MATERIALS: Medium to heavyweight furnishing fabric, lining fabric, interlining, matching threads, goblet pleat heading tape, leadweight tape, track or pole

FABRIC: Follow the instructions for measuring the window and calculating fabric quantities (see pages 22-23), allowing 10cm (4in) for the hem and the width of the chosen heading tape for the top edge. Allow extra for pattern match. You will need the same amount of interlining as main curtain fabric and enough lining fabric to make up to finished curtain size. Use measurement W (see pages 22-23) to give you the amount of heading tape you require. The length of leadweight should be the length of the finished curtain hems.

1 First cut out lengths of the main fabric and interlining using the measurements that you have made. Cut the lining to the finished curtain size. Join widths of main fabric and lining (see steps 1 and 2, pages 36-37).

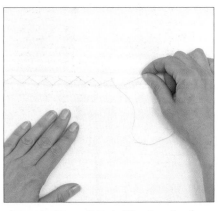

2 To join widths of interlining, place two lengths side by side on a large flat surface, overlap the joining edges by about 1.25cm (½in). Use herringbone stitch (see pages 78-79) to join the widths together. Continue in the same way until all widths needed to make up the curtain size are joined.

3 Lay the interlining out flat and place the main fabric, right side up, on top. Pin the two materials together down the centre from top to bottom. Fold back the fabric to this centre pinned line and lockstitch to the interlining down the centre (see pages 78-79). Smooth the fabric back over interlining for 38cm (15in) and lockstitch together again in a line parallel to the first. Continue in this way until you reach the curtain edge. Tack the two materials together down the side. Repeat in the same way from the centre to the opposite edge.

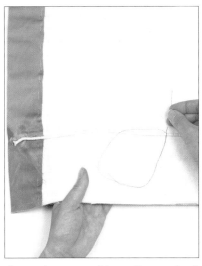

4 Down each side fold in a single 5cm (2in) hem to the wrong side. Turn up a 10cm (4in) single hem along the lower edge and press in place. Open out the hem, lay the length of leadweight tape along the pressed hem line and stitch in place at intervals. Mitre the hem corners (see pages 82-83), slipstitch the angled mitre seam, then herringbone all the raw hem edges to hold.

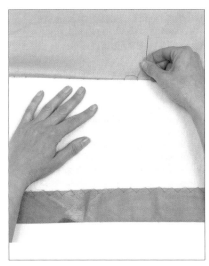

5 Place the lining over the interlined main fabric, with wrong sides together. Pin down the centre and lockstitch lining to interlining across the curtain (see step 3), finishing each line just above the hem edge. Leave the side edges unstitched. Trim the lining fabric at the edges if necessary so that the raw edges are flush with the finished main curtain edges.

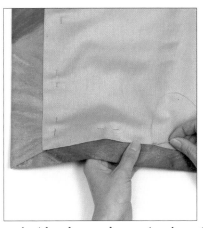

6 Turn under a single 5cm (2in) hem along the lower lining edge and a 2.5cm (1in) hem down each side edge, and press in place. Create a mock mitre on the lining hem corners (see pages 82-83). Press lining hem edges and slipstitch the lining in place to the curtain fabric side and lower hems.

7 Before adding the heading tape, check the length of the curtains carefully. Then turn in the top edge and stitch on heading tape (see pages 28-29). Pull up cords in heading tape and attach a covered button to each pleat point. Secure the cords on a cord tidy and hang the curtains.

Scalloped heading

Scalloped headings create a decorative top edge and are suitable for unlined or light-lined curtains. The size of scallop depends on the length of the curtain. For full-length curtains allow a scallop width of between 13-15cm (5-6in) and a depth equal to half the width measurement. On a short curtain, scallops will look better if they are smaller.

This curtain is hung from fabric ties sewn in place between the main curtain fabric and the facing. For an easy alternative, use lengths of ribbon instead of the fabric ties.

MATERIALS: Medium-weight furnishing or sheer fabric, medium-weight iron-on interfacing matching thread, pole or rod, card for pattern

FABRIC: Fix the hanging system in place and measure from the underside to the sill or floor level. Allow one-and-a-half times the pole length. Follow the instructions (pages 22-23) for calculating quantities fabric quantities. For full length curtains allow a strip for the top facing 13cm (5in) by the width of the curtain. Cut the interfacing 10cm (4in) wide by the width of the curtain. For each tie, you will need a 75cm (30in) length of fabric twice the required width plus 2.5cm (1in).

1 Cut out and make up the curtain width (see steps 1 and 2, pages 28-29). Stitch 2.5 (1in) side hems (see step 3, pages 28-29) but leave the top 13cm (5in) unstitched. Iron the length of interfacing to the wrong side of the top of the curtain, matching it up with the top and side edges.

2 Along the lower edge of the facing turn under a single 1.25cm (½in) hem to the wrong side and stitch. With right sides together, pin the facing to the curtain top edge with raw edges matching. Stitch down the side edges, matching the side hems. Tack along the top edge and press but do not stitch.

3 Mark the scallop positions on the top edge of the fabric. The scallops and spaces between, which should be slightly wider than the width of the fabric ties, need to work out equally across the width of the curtain, with a space for a tie at each end. Position a scallop in the centre of the curtain.

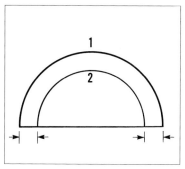

4 Make card templates for the scallop shape. Cut (1), using a saucer or compass as a guide. Cut a second template 2.5cm (1in) narrower than the first (2). This indicates the cutting line.

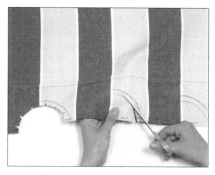

5 Line up the larger template (1) with each marked position for a scallop shape and draw in. Position the smaller template (2) centrally in the marked scallop shape, lining up the straight top edge with the curtain edge and draw in shape. Tack, then stitch each scallop separately. Cut out the scallops, following the cutting line and notch into the curved seam allowance.

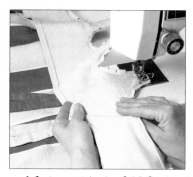

6 Fold each tie strip in half lengthways, with right side inside, and stitch down the long edge and across one end. Turn right side out, turn in the raw short end and slipstitch closed. Fold each tie in half and place the ties between the main fabric and facing with the fold flush with the top straight edge. Stitch across each straight top edge 1.25cm (½in) from the raw edge. Press, turn curtain right side out and press again. Slipstitch lower facing edge to the main curtain fabric.

7 To finish the curtain, first hang it, tie the fabric ties and turn up the lower hem. Remove and stitch the lower hem. Rehang the curtain.

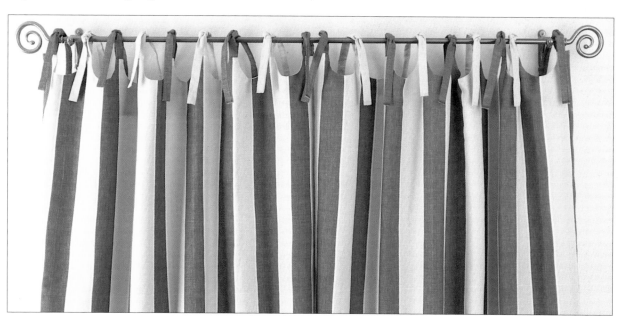

Curtain Dressing

The addition of a valance, pelmet or even a simple tieback can make an ordinary window treatment more sophisticated.

Tiebacks serve a practical purpose, holding curtains away from a window when they are drawn back, as well as creating an additional decorative element. They can be made in both classic and contemporary styles.

A valance, pelmet, modern draped heading and traditionally arranged swags and tails are positioned above a pair of curtains or a blind, hiding the top of the treatment and creating a neater overall finish.

This chapter contains

Classic tiebacks

A shaped and stiffened tieback, that widens towards the centre and curves to follow the curtain's gathers, is the classic way to hold back curtains.

Tiebacks are usually positioned one third from the top of the curtain, half-way down the curtain or one third from its lower edge, depending on the shape of the window.

MATERIALS: Furnishing fabric or fabric and lining, matching thread, tieback iron-on interfacing, paper for template, cord for shaped tieback, button shape for scalloped tieback, rings and hooks for fixing

FABRIC: First measure for the tieback length required. Enlarge the template to the required size (see pages 90-91). For each tieback you will need two pieces of fabric this size (or one of fabric and one of lining), plus a 1.25cm (½in) seam allowance, and one piece of interfacing the size of each finished tieback. Measure along the outside edge of the pattern for the length of cord you will need for the corded tieback and add 5cm (2in).

CORDED TIEBACK

1 Decide where to place the tieback, trying alternative positions with a length of string or fabric. Lightly mark in pencil where the fixing is to go. Hold a tape measure around the curtain from this marked point to assess the tieback length. The tape measurement is the length of your finished tieback. Screw in hooks into the wall.

3 Place the interfacing piece centrally on the wrong side of the front tieback fabric and iron in place following the manufacturer's instructions. When the interfacing is attached, clip into the seam allowance, then press fabric allowance on to the wrong side of the tieback, covering the edge of the interfacing, and tack in place.

2 Enlarge template A on a photocopier (see pages 90-91) and placing the fold edge on folded paper, cut out a full size pattern. Using the tieback pattern, cut out the tieback interfacing. Then cut two pieces of fabric plus 1.25cm (½in) all round for the seam allowance.

4 Press the seam allowance on the lining to the wrong side, clipping the allowance to make it lie flat. With tieback right side down, place the lining, right side up to cover the interfacing. Match edges, then slipstitch together leaving a 2.5cm (1in) gap at one end of the tieback. Slip the end of the cord into the gap, then slipstitch it around the edge of the tieback. To finish, tuck the opposite cord end into the gap, stitch cord ends together and slipstitch the opening closed. Attach a curtain ring to each end of the tieback and hang.

SCALLOP-EDGED TIEBACK

1 Work out the tieback size and cut out a pattern (see steps 1 and 2, Corded Tieback) using template B (see pages 90-91).

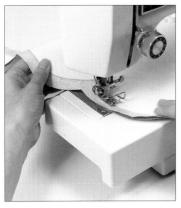

2 Cut out the interfacing, lining and main fabric, then attach the interfacing to the wrong side of the fabric (see step 3, Corded Tieback). Place the lining over the main fabric, with right sides together, and stitch 1.25cm (½in) from the raw edges along the lower scalloped edge. Trim into the seam allowance around the inner points and curves turn right side out and press. Turn in the raw edges and slipstitch closed. Make a self-cover button and stitch it to the tieback. Stitch rings in place then hang the tieback.

Creative tiebacks

A quick and easy way to create your own decorative tieback is to use curtain heading tape. Match up with a gathered heading tape used to make the curtains or choose from smocked, lattice or trellis tape for an ornate finish.

For a three dimensional look it is very simple to make twisted tiebacks from padded tubes of fabric that complement the curtains.

MATERIALS:

Gathered tieback: Furnishing fabric, lattice heading tape, matching thread, dressmaker's pencil, rings and tieback hooks

Twisted tieback: Furnishing fabric, wadding, matching thread, rings and tieback hooks

FABRIC:

Gathered tieback: Measure the tieback length required (see step 1, pages 44-45). Allow 2½ times this length for each tieback and two pieces of fabric the width of the heading tape plus 2.5cm (1in) for each tieback. For heading tape allow the ungathered length, plus 10cm (5in) for positioning.

Twisted tieback: For each tieback cut the fabric strip 10cm (4in) wide and 2¼ times the finished length plus 2.5cm (1in). Cut two wadding strips 7.5cm (3in) wide and 2¼ times the finished length.

GATHERED TIEBACK

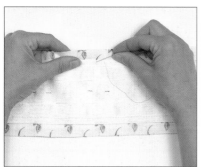
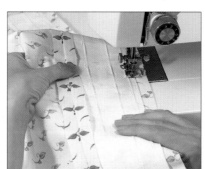
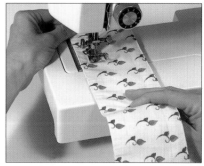

1 Make the length required for each tieback piece, joining strips with open seams. Then, with right sides facing and all edges matching, pin the two tieback pieces together. Centre the heading tape over the tieback pieces and pin in position. Secure the cords at one end of the tape and at the other pull them free. Cut the tape to fit. Tack all three sections together along one long edge only.

2 Stitch along the tacked long edge close to the heading tape edge. Open out the joined lengths and press the seam open. Stitch the tape in place along the other long edge, attaching it to one tieback piece only, then press the seam allowance over the edge of the heading tape. On the other long edge, press under a 1.25cm (½in) hem to the wrong side. Match finished long edges and slipstitch closed.

3 Turn in the fabric at the end of the tape where the cords are tied and slipstitch closed. Then with a dressmaker's pencil draw two lines along the length of the tieback 2cm (3/4in) from each side edge. Machine along these lines. This gives the tieback a neat finish. Gather the tieback to the finished length. Turn in the final raw end and slipstitch closed. Attach a curtain ring to each end of the tieback.

TWISTED TIEBACK

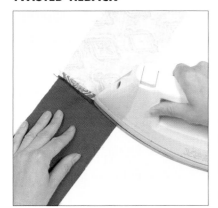

1 Cut out the fabric strips from two fabrics. To join the strips, place one strip on top of the other, with right sides together and all edges matching. Stitch across one short end 1.25cm (½in) from the raw edge. Press seam open to form one double length strip of two different fabrics 10cm (4in) wide.

2 Make the tube by placing the strip wrong side uppermost, turn in and press along one raw edge by 1.5cm (⅝in). Place the wadding centrally on top and bring both long edges of the fabric to the centre, pinning the folded edge over the raw edge to form a tube around the wadding. Slipstitch the pinned edge to hold it in place. Trim the wadding, turn in the raw edge at each end and tack closed.

3 To twist the strip, fold in half at the join and stitch across, 1.25cm (½in) from the fold. Turn the edges to the back, forming a point and slip stitch in place. Attach a curtain ring. Twist the two lengths together evenly, with the seam at the back. Pin ends to hold. Check for length, then stitch the ends together in a point as before and attach a ring to this tieback end.

Valances

Unlike a pelmet which is usually flat and stiffened, a valance has a gathered heading and is constructed like a curtain. It can be embellished in a number of ways that include a bound edge, a frill, a border of complementary fabric or a fringe. A valance will also hide an unattractive curtain top or track and completes the decorative effect of a window treatment.

MATERIALS: *Gathered valance:* Furnishing lining and fabric, fabric for border, matching threads, heading tape, valance rail
Pleated valance: Furnishing fabric, lining fabric, matching thread, heading tape, valance rail

FABRIC: Work out fabric and lining quantities as for curtains (see pages 22-23). The length should be about one sixth the length of the curtains
Gathered valance: For heading tape allow two and a half times the finished length plus 10cm (4in)
Pleated valance: For heading tape allow three times the finished length plus 10cm (4in)

GATHERED VALANCE

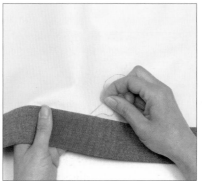

1 To join fabric widths, cut the widths of fabric to the valance length. Turn to the wrong side and stitch as open seams 1.25cm (½in) from raw edge (see pages 80-81). On patterned fabric tack together from the right side using ladder stitch (see pages 78-79).Make each lining length 8cm (3in) shorter than the top fabric and with right sides facing, join widths as for valance fabric. Trim 1.25cm (½in) off each lining side edge.

2 Place lining and fabric together with right sides facing. Match one side edge and position the lining 8cm (3in) below the fabric top edge and parallel to it. Tack, then stitch the side seams 1.25cm (½in) from raw edge. Tack together along lining top edge. Place border and valance with right sides facing, raw edges matching and 1.25cm (½in) overlapping at each short end; stitch in place. Press over border raw edge to the valance back and slipstitch. Turn in raw ends and slipstitch closed.

3 To attach the heading tape, fold over the fabric top edge to the wrong side to form a single hem, covering the lining top edge. Press in position and place the tape over this single hem just below the top edge and covering the fabric raw edge. Allow a 5cm (2in) overlap of tape at each end. Tack to hold. Stitch the heading tape in place (see Step 5 pages 28-29). Draw up the gathers, arranging them evenly and fit to the valance rail.

PLEATED VALANCE

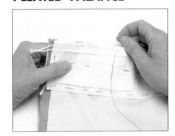

1 Allowing three times the finished length, cut out fabric and lining and join together, following step 1 Gathered Valance. Turn up the hem. Tack the pleated heading tape in position, allowing a 5cm (2in) overlap of tape at each end. Turn under the overlap, knot and turn under the cords at one end and pull the three cords through to the front at the other. Stitch in place all round.

2 To draw up the pleats take the cords at the end of the heading tape and pull them through. The pleats will be drawn into place as the cords are pulled and the top cord will hold the pleats in place. When all the pleats are drawn up, knot the cord ends to secure. Check pleats are even and press the pleats in position for a crisp finish. Fit the valance to the rail with curtain hooks.

Pelmet

A pelmet, a strip of stiffened fabric fixed to a shelf above the curtain track, gives an ornate finish to a window treatment.

A pelmet former (stiffener), which has printed pelmet shapes in a range of sizes on the backing paper, makes construction easy. The main fabric is simply smoothed on to one side of the stiffener, turned to the back and then the lining is added over the adhesive on the opposite side.

Before making the pelmet, fix a pelmet shelf to the wall using the same technique as for fixing a batten (see pages 60-61). The shelf should be made from 2cm (¾in) thick ply 10cm (4in) wide and be 5cm (2in) longer than the curtain track. Position the shelf so that it is 5cm (2in) above the curtain and secure with L-shaped brackets at 20cm (8in) intervals.

MATERIALS: Medium-weight furnishing fabric, lining fabric, 60cm (24in) wide double-sided self-adhesive pelmet stiffener, matching threads, pelmet shelf, self-adhesive grip tape fastening (Velcro), dressmaker's pencil

FABRIC: To calculate the total width of fabric required, fix the pelmet shelf (see pages 60-61), then measure the front and side edges of the shelf and add 5cm (2in) to this measurement for the pelmet width. Make the pelmet template (see step 1, below), measure its depth and add 5cm (2in). Calculate the number of fabric widths needed, dividing the total width required by the fabric width measurement, then multiply this by the pelmet depth measurement. You will need a piece of fabric and a piece of lining this size, and pelmet stiffener to the pelmet depth by the total fabric width and grip tape fastening equal to the total fabric width.

1 To create a shaped edge, either follow one of the designs on the back of the self-adhesive stiffener or use the grid printed on the backing paper to make your own.
Measure the length of the pelmet shelf, including the sides. Mark on the grid vertical lines to show the point where the front of the pelmet meets the side edges and also mark the centre front of the pelmet. Here, a zigzag edge 20cm (8in) deep and 18.5cm (7¼in) wide has been used.

2 Join fabric widths if required, positioning a full width of fabric in the centre and part widths at the outside edges. Press the fabric, then mark the centre point on the wrong side. Position the template centrally on the wrong side of the fabric, matching centre marks, and draw around it with a dressmaker's pencil. Mark a second line 2.5cm (1in) outside the first and cut out the fabric following this line. Use the fabric as a template to cut out a piece of lining fabric.

3 On one side of the stiffener, lift the backing paper at the centre slightly, then cut vertically through the paper only. This allows you to fit one half of the stiffener at a time. Working from the centre, peel back a short section of the backing paper and smooth the stiffener over the wrong side of the fabric. Remove only a small area of backing at a time. Repeat with the second half of the stiffener.

4 Clip or notch into the seam allowance on corners and curves, then peel off the backing paper on the reverse of the stiffener and smooth the allowance on to the opposite side of the stiffener. On the lining, press under a 2.5cm (1in) hem to the wrong side, then gently smooth the lining, right side up, in place on the stiffener. Slipstitch the lining to the fabric around the edge to hold.

5 To fit the pelmet, attach the hooked side of the self-adhesive grip tape fastening strip to the pelmet shelf edge. Then fix the opposite strip to the pelmet lining fabric along the top edge. Crease the pelmet strip to match the shelf corners, then press the touch-and-close fastening strips together.

Draped headings

A length of single-width fabric, draped over a curtain pole or metal holdbacks, balances well with the simple lines of a Roman or roller blind or can be used on its own to make a decorative frame for a window or doorway.

The two examples of a draped heading illustrated here can be made in the minimum of time and require almost no sewing.

MATERIALS:

Draped curtain poles: Lightweight furnishing fabric, matching thread, pole and fixings, café clips
Archway drape: Sheer fabric, matching thread, three metal holdbacks and fixings

FABRIC:

Archway drape: Choose a fabric without a one way design. Fix the holdbacks (see step 1 below), then use string to check the drape depth and length. Measure the string for the length of fabric. Allow 5cm (2in) extra for hem allowance.
Draped curtain poles: Fix the pole in place and measure for the length of fabric in the same way as for a single drape.

DRAPED CURTAIN POLES

1 Fix the pole in place (see pages 20-21). Depending on how much of the window top you wish the swags to cover, place it between 10-20cm (4-8in) above the window.

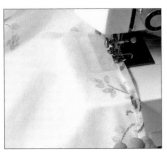

2 Cut the selvages off the fabric, then turn under a 1.25cm (½in) double hem to the wrong side on all raw edges. To create wedge shaped tails, cut the fabric ends on the bias before stitching.

3 To create even length tails loop the fabric over the pole starting from the centre with equal lengths on either side. Secure with curtain clips. Loosely arrange the swirls of fabric to each pole end, making sure the tails are the same length before securing. Arrange the fabric to cover the clips.

ARCHWAY DRAPE

1 Begin by fixing the metal holdbacks to the wall. Place the central holdback well above the door or window and the side holdbacks about 8-13cm (3-5in) above the doorway or window and the same distance out to each side, depending on the width of the fabric.

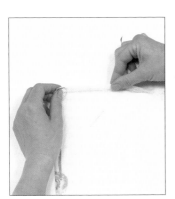

2 Cut the selvages off the fabric, then turn in narrow double hems to the wrong side on all raw edges and stitch to secure. Hand stitching will be less obvious on sheer fabrics.

3 Fold the length of fabric in half to find the centre, then loop this around the top holdback, keeping the right side of the fabric to the front. Arrange fabric in a swag to each side and secure by looping around the side holdbacks.

Swags and tails

Classic design swags and tails are made in three pieces, with the swag and tails made separately and fixed to a pelmet shelf above the window. The tails, cut at a sharp angle, are carefully arranged to hang in deep pleats that show the complementary lining as well as the top fabric.

Here we show a simple design of one swag and two tails that fall in two pleats on either side but for a more ornate effect you can, following these instructions, increase the swags and add extra pleats to the tails.

MATERIALS: Old sheets for the pattern, furnishing fabric, lining, matching thread, pelmet shelf, staple gun or hammer and tacks, self-adhesive grip tape fastening (Velcro)

FABRIC: Fix the pelmet shelf (see pages 60-61 Roman Blind) and cut the covering to this size. Measure the finished pattern for the fabric quantity and allow 2cm (3/4in) seam allowances on all sides. Allow for pattern matching if necessary. You will need the same amount of lining as fabric.

1 Cut the pelmet shelf cover fabric to the pelmet shelf measurement plus a 2cm (¾in) seam allowance. Mark the centre and corner points. To work out the design for the swag, tack or staple the sheeting to the topside of the shelf. Arrange a central swag to your chosen depth, secure this and pleat up the fabric at each end, pinning the pleats in place. Mark the central point and the pleat folds and then cut off the excess sheeting leaving a 2cm (¾in) seam allowance.

2 Measure the desired tail length, these are usually between one and two thirds of the curtain length. Cut two pieces of sheeting to this length, cutting the lower edge on the bias to form a narrowing tail. With the longer edge on the outside, staple or tack one tail pattern around the corner of the pelmet shelf, masking the swag end. Arrange the pleats, pin and mark the pleat positions on the top and lower edges. Repeat this as a mirror-image on the other side.

3 To make up the top swag, cut fabric and lining pieces, following your pattern and allowing a 2cm (¾in) seam allowance on all sides, the pleat folds will show as zigzag edges. Place fabric and lining with right sides together and stitch along front and back edges only. Turn right side out and press. Mark the central point with a pin. Press in the marked pleats and tack in place. Check the effect and then tack together the raw edges.

4 To make up the tails cut out from fabric and lining using both patterns and allowing a 2cm (¾in) seam allowance on all sides. For each tail, place lining and fabric pieces with right sides together and stitch along the sides and lower edges. Clip the corners, turn right side out and press. Do the same with the other tail piece. Fold in the pleats on each tail, as marked on the pattern, and then tack along the top edge.

5 With right sides together and matching the central points, pin the swag top edge to the pelmet cover front edge. Pin the tails around each corner in the same way. Place over the pelmet board, check the effect and adjust if necessary. Remove. Place wrong side to the pelmet cover and stitch, 2cm (¾in) from all raw edges. Trim the seam allowance and clip the corners. Press and re-hang, fixing the pelmet cover in place with grip tape (Velcro) or staples.

Before you Begin: Blinds

Blinds, a versatile alternative to curtains, can be raised during the day or, when made from finer fabrics, left down to provide privacy.

Though the amount of fabric required is dependent on the style of blind chosen, the simpler styles of blind use a lot less fabric than curtains. They do not, however, provide the same amount of insulation. If extra insulation is required consider using both a blind and curtains on the same window.

This chapter introduces the principal types of blind, shows how to put up an appropriate hanging system, and gives all the information needed to measure up accurately and calculate the quantities of fabric and materials required.

Blind styles

Different blinds suit different situations and types of fabric. Here are some tips on how they work, areas or windows for which they are specially suitable, fabrics to choose and final finishing touches you can apply.

ROLLER BLIND

◄ A roller blind is the simplest form of blind. It uses a minimum amount of fabric and rolls up into a narrow strip at the top of the window, allowing the maximum amount of light into a room. Roller blinds are a practical choice for kitchen and bathroom windows, or for use at a window with a beautiful view. The simple shape of the blind also lends itself to the addition of a decoratively shaped edge.

ROMAN BLIND

◄ A Roman blind lies flat to the window in the same way as a roller blind. However, cords threaded through rings on tapes at the back of the blind create neat horizontal pleats when it is pulled up. This type of blind is suitable for use in most rooms and can be made from closely woven medium-weight fabrics or from sheer fabric. Borders at the side and lower edges give a sophisticated finish and are a good way to add width if the fabric is narrower than the window. Roman blinds also look effective when teamed with curtains made in a complementary fabric.

FESTOON BLIND

◄ The ultimate in romance, a festoon blind is gathered both horizontally and vertically. This type of blind is often used to give privacy during the day or provide some shade in a sunny room and is most often made from sheer fabrics or fine fabrics like polyester-cotton. The ruched effect of a festoon blind looks best outlined with a frill.

AUSTRIAN BLIND

◄ An Austrian blind, which hangs in curtain-like gathers and then falls into deep swags at the lower edge, creates a grand effect ideally suited to living rooms and bedrooms. Austrian blinds can be lined or unlined. For a decorative finish, trim the lower edge with fringes and frills.

Hanging blinds

Blinds are fixed in place in a number of different ways depending on the type of blind and the fixing you decide to use.

ROLLER BLIND

Roller blinds are the simplest type of blind to fit. The kit includes brackets to take the roller, which must be fixed on either side of the window. The blind is fixed to the roller which then fits back into the brackets.

1 Buy a blind kit to fit the space. Fix the blind brackets to the wall, checking the manufacturer's instructions to ensure that the left and right brackets are correctly placed. Allow 2.5-4cm (1-1⅜in) above the brackets for the thickness of fabric around the pole. Mark the positions for the screws square with the window, and fix the brackets in place (see pages 20-21).

2 Measure the distance between the brackets and then check this measurement against the length of the roller. If necessary, cut the roller to size by sawing off the bare timber end. Place the cap over the sawn end and gently hammer the pin in place through the centre. Check the roller fit again by placing it in the brackets.

ROMAN BLIND

Roman blinds are fixed in place to a batten above a window. Screw eyes, positioned along the underside of the batten to line up with the vertical tapes on the blind, are used to take the lengths of cord to one side of the window so that the blind can be raised or lowered easily.

2 Position the brackets about 4cm (1⅜in) from each end of the batten, flush with the back edge. Mark the position of the fixing holes and screw the brackets to the batten. Holding the batten, with the attached brackets, against the two pencil marks on the fixing surface, check with a spirit level that the batten is horizontal.

1 Decide where to position the blind and mark this on the wall or timber surface lightly in pencil. Measure this distance, then cut a batten to length. Sand the sawn end and check the fit. If the blind is to fit in a recessed window, the batten should just slip neatly into the space.

Then mark the position of the screw holes for the brackets on the wall or woodwork. Take the batten down and remove the screws securing it to the brackets. Fix the brackets in place at the window following your marked positions (see pages 20-21). Once in place, the brackets can be painted.

FESTOON AND AUSTRIAN BLINDS

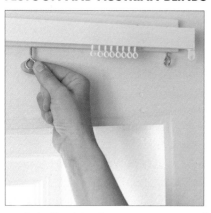

The simplest method of fixing a festoon or Austrian blind is to use the special blind track that comes with integral cord holders. This type of track is fixed in the same way as ordinary curtain track (see pages 12-13). Alternatively, you can put up a batten with a simple curtain track mounted on the front of it and with screw eyes fixed underneath to take the cords out to the side (see Roman blind).

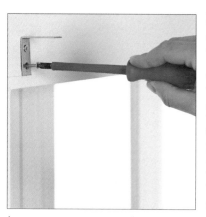

Measure the distance that the batten is to cover and then cut the batten to length. Fix the brackets as for a Roman blind. Cut a length of curtain track to fit the front of the batten. Screw the track brackets to the batten and then fit the track with the curtain hooks and an end stop at each end. Once the blind is complete, position the screw eyes along the lower edge of the batten to match up with the vertical tape positions.

Calculating quantities

Most blinds are either made to fit within a window recess or if the window is flush with the wall to cover the window. Blinds for flush windows are usually made slightly larger than the window to prevent light appearing around the blind edges, though they can also be made significantly wider or longer than the window if required.

MEASURING UP
Recessed window

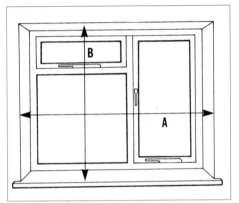

To fit into a recess a blind should be 1.25cm (½in) smaller than the recess, on each side. The fabric for the blind is cut slightly narrower than the batten.

First measure the recess width and deduct 2cm (¾in). Call this measurement A. Then measure from the top of the recess to the window sill and deduct 1.25cm (½in). Call this measurement B.

Flush window

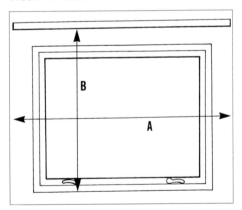

Measure the width of the window from the outer edge of the frame on either side, then add 10cm (4in). Call this measurement A.

Then measure from the hanging system to the lower frame edge and add 10cm (4in). Call this measurement B.

If you prefer to make a blind that sits above the sill, omit the extra 10cm (4in).

FABRIC AND MATERIAL REQUIREMENTS
Festoon blind

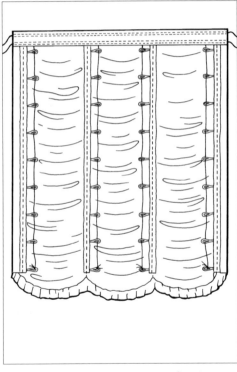

Fabric: twice measurement A, for the length allow one and a half times measurement B. *Heading tape:* twice fabric width A plus 10cm (4in) . *Festoon blind tape:* fabric length, by the number of vertical tapes. *Cord:* twice measurement B plus measurement A, by the number of vertical tapes.
Blind track: measurement A. *Rings:* One for each vertical tape.

Roman blind

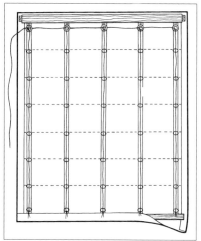

Fabric: measurement A plus 8cm (3in) by B plus 13cm (5in). *Lining:* measurement A by B less 5cm (2in). *Roman blind tape:* measurement B, by the number of vertical tapes. *Cord:* twice measurement B plus measurement A, by the number of vertical tapes. *Griptape (Velcro):* measurement A. *Batten:* One batten 40x 20mm (1¾ x ¾) by measurement A. *L-shaped brackets:* Two brackets 45 x 45mm (1¾ x 1¾in). Allow more for batten longer than 1.20m (4ft). *Lath:* One lath 25 x 6mm (1 x ¼in) by measurement A. *Rings:* One for each vertical tape. *Screw eyes:* One screw eye for each vertical tape.

Austrian blind

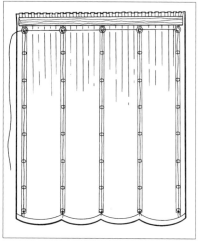

Fabric: two to two-and-a-half times measurement A multiplied by B plus 40-50cm (16-20in). *Lining:* fabric width less 5cm (2in) by the fabric length less heading tape depth and 2.5cm (1in). *Blind track:* measurement A. *Heading tape:* fabric width plus 10cm (4in). *Austrian blind tape:* fabric length, by the number of vertical tapes. *Cord:* twice measurement B plus measurement A, by the number of vertical tapes. *Rings:* One for each vertical tape used. If using rings only you will need one for each vertical pleat on each drawn horizontal line it crosses plus edges (see pages 72-73).

Roller blind

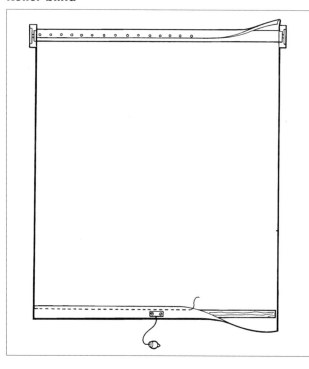

Fabric: the length of the roller plus 5cm (2in) by measurement B plus 30cm (12in). Allow extra for a shaped edge. *Roller Blind Kit:* measurement A or the next size up if not available.

JOINING FABRIC WIDTHS

For blinds that need more than one length of fabric to make up the width simply multiply the measurement for the length by the number of widths to find the amount of fabric required.

If you choose a fabric with a design that needs to be matched across the width you will need to allow extra. The retailer will check the pattern repeat and help you to calculate the amount of extra fabric required. A bold motif looks best if it is centred on a blind, so allow for this as well.

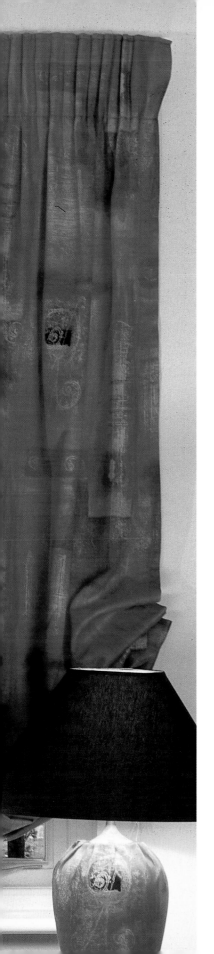

Making Blinds

This chapter gives step-by-step instructions on how to make a variety of blinds, from a simple roller blind to romantic festoon or more elaborate Austrian and Roman blinds.

Soft blinds are made from a rectangle of fabric that is prepared in much the same way as a curtain and can be lined or unlined. Austrian, Roman and festoon blinds have vertical tapes positioned on the reverse side and it is the way in which these are gathered that creates the different effects.

Blinds are the ideal treatment for a window where you want to introduce the maximum amount of light or enjoy the view. Most blinds use less fabric than curtains but they also provide less insulation. The ultimate window treatment is to combine curtains and blinds for a decorative, practical solution.

Roller blind

Simple in shape, roller blinds look effective when made from a fabric with a bold design and finished with a decorative edge.

Pre-stiffened fabric is the best choice for a roller blind as it comes in a range of wide widths (joined widths of fabric are not satisfactory for roller blinds), and can be wiped clean. Alternatively, use a closely woven cotton, treated with fabric stiffener.

Fix the brackets at the top of the window before you start (see pages 60-61) and cut the roller to fit.

MATERIALS: Pre-stiffened blind fabric or closely woven cotton treated with fabric stiffener, matching thread, roller blind kit, double-sided self adhesive tape, tacks and a hammer or staples and staple gun

FABRIC: Follow the instructions for measuring the window and calculating the quantities of fabric and materials required (see pages 62-63).

1 Lay the fabric out flat, centring the design. With a dressmaker's pencil, mark the cutting lines. Check that the corners form accurate right angles (see pages 24-25) and then cut out.

2 On woven cotton use a zigzag stitch to neaten the side and top edges (hems stop the blind from rolling up smoothly). On pre-stiffened fabric this should not be necessary.

3 Cut a decorative edge, following the fabric's design. Form a channel at the back of the blind above the shaped edge, wide enough to take the lath, and machine stitch in place close to the folded edge. Slot the lath into the casing and stitch across the ends to close. On the wrong side of the blind mark the centre point of the lath. Fix the cord holder through the fabric and into the lath at the marked position.

4 To fix the blind to the roller, mark a straight line along the roller and attach a narrow strip of double-sided tape. Lay the blind down, right side up and place the roller across the top with the spring mechanism on your left. Partially roll the fabric around the roller so that the fabric edge matches the tape edge and press down along the tape to hold. Fix with tacks or staples, at about 2.5cm (1in) intervals.

5 To hang the blind, first roll it up and place the roller in the brackets with the blind fully rolled up. Pull the blind down, then give a quick tug down to release the stop and allow it to roll up. If the spring is not fully tensioned the blind will not roll up correctly. In this case remove the blind, roll up again and repeat. This time the blind should roll up on its own.

STRAIGHT-EDGED BLIND
To create a blind with a straight lower edge, neaten the lower raw edge with zigzag stitch, then turn up a single hem wide enough to take the lath. Press in the fold with your fingers, and stitch across the width close to the raw edge.

Roman blind

When pulled up, a Roman blind forms neat horizontal pleats. This effect is achieved by cords threaded through rings or loops on rows of vertical tapes running across the back of the blind (see pages 58-59).

Before making the blind, fix the brackets in place at the window (see pages 60-61) and paint both the brackets and the batten to match the window frame.

MATERIALS: Closely woven cotton fabric, lining fabric, matching threads, Roman blind tape, blind cord, screw eyes, self-adhesive griptape fastening (Velcro), batten, L-shaped brackets, lath, cleat and screws for fixing

FABRIC: Follow the instructions for measuring the window and calculating the quantities of fabric and materials required (see pages 62-63)

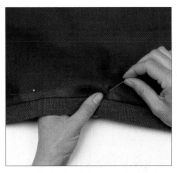

1 Make up the required width of fabric, making any joins with open seams (see pages 80-81) and matching the design across widths. Stitch the lining in the same way. Pin the fabric and lining together with right sides facing, matching the side edges and stitch 1.25cm (½in) from the raw edge. The fabric, will be wider than the lining. Press the seams open, then turn right side out.

2 Use a pin to mark the centre point on both the lining and fabric at the top and bottom edges. With lining uppermost, line up the pins, then press the side edges with equal overlap of the top fabric on either side edge of the lining. Turn up the lower hem on the top fabric so that hem edge sits over lining raw edge. Press well but do not stitch.

3 Working from the back of the blind, position a tape vertically to cover the left-hand seamline. Place the lower edge of the tape just inside the hem edge and the first ring (loop) position just above it, tack in place. Repeat on the opposite side, ensuring that the ring (loop) positions line up exactly across the blind.

4 Position the rest of the tapes at equal intervals of 22-28cm (8½-11in) across the blind, lining up the ring (loop) positions, wider spaces will result in drooping. Tack tape to the blind and stitch down either side, close to the edge. For pleat definition, stitch horizontal lines across the blind at each ring (loop) position.

5 On the lower edge, turn up the hem to the pressed line and turn under the hem to the wrong side. Stitch hem in place, encasing tape raw ends. Slipstitch one hem end closed, push the lath into the hem from the far end, then slipstitch this end closed.

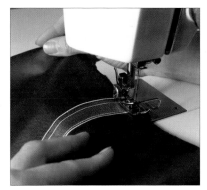

6 Zigzag stitch fabric and lining together along the top raw edge. Press a strip of self-adhesive griptape fastening flush with the edge and stitch in place. Press the other half of the griptape on to the front of the batten, flush with the top edge. Fix the blind in place. With a bradawl, mark screw eye positions on the underside of the batten lining up with each tape. Screw the eyes home.

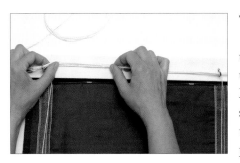

7 If looped tape is used, fix a ring to the tape just above the hem edge. Secure the cord end to the hem edge ring, then thread it through the rings (loops). At the top of the tape thread the cord along the screw eyes on the batten and out to one side. Make sure all the cord lengths lie to one side of the blind. Then screw the batten in place to the fixed brackets and fix the cleat at the side of the window to match the cords. Tie cords together and pull up the blind.

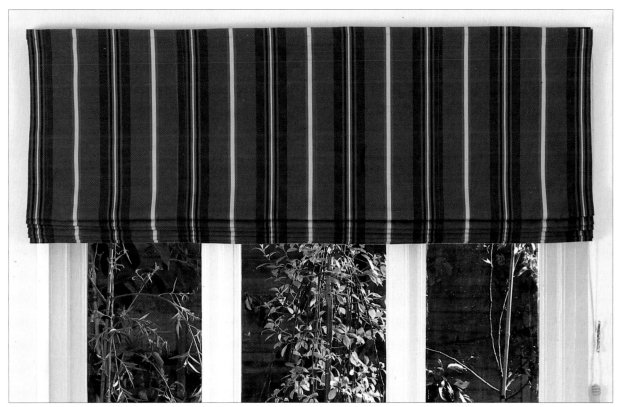

Festoon blind

A festoon blind, which is gathered both horizontally and vertically even when lowered, looks best when made up in sheer or very fine fabrics.

The blind shown here is made to hang from a special blind track that comes with integral cord holders. This track is fixed to the wall in the same way as ordinary curtain track (see pages 20-21).

MATERIALS: Sheer fabric, transparent curtain heading tape, blind track, festoon blind tape, nylon cord, small transparent curtain rings, matching threads, cleat and screws for fixing

FABRIC: Follow the instructions for measuring the windows and calculating the quantities of fabric and materials required (see pages 62-63). If adding a frill, calculate the extra fabric required (see pages 82-83) and add this to fabric quantities.

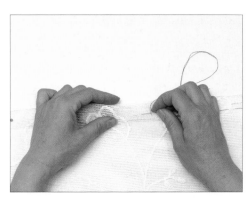

1 Make up the required width of fabric, joining widths together with French seams (see pages 80-81). Match the design across widths on patterned fabrics (see pages 24-25). Then turn in a single 2.5cm (1in) hem down each side edge and tack to hold.

2 With the fabric wrong side up, pin one strip of festoon blind tape vertically over each side hem just covering the raw fabric edge of the hem with the first loop 5cm (2in) from the lower raw edge of the fabric. The loops along the tape should lie towards the centre of the blind.

Position more vertical tape lengths, in the same way, across the blind at equally spaced intervals of 40cm-60cm (16in-24in), covering seams where possible. At the bottom end of each tape pull the cords to the back of the tape and knot to secure. Stitch each tape down the centre. Attach one transparent ring to the loop near the bottom of each tape.

3 To add a frill, first cut strips and make up the frill (see pages 84-85). Pull up the gathering threads evenly to fit the lower edge of the blind and, with wrong sides facing, stitch the frill 5mm (¼in) from the edge attaching vertical tape ends in the seam. Turn to the right side, refold, press and stitch 1cm (⅜in) from the seamed edge as a French seam (see pages 80-81).

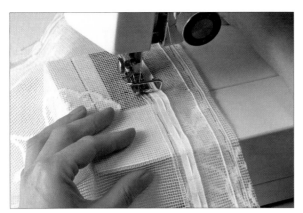

5 Draw up each vertical tape to the finished blind length and knot. Don't cut cords but wind them around the cord tidy. Arrange gathers evenly.

4 On the top edge, turn under a 2.5cm (1in) hem to the wrong side and place the transparent curtain heading tape 5mm (¼in) from the top edge. Trim the top end of each vertical tape so that it will just tuck under the heading tape lower edge. Pull out the cords on the vertical tapes so that they hang free below the heading tape, then stitch the heading tape in position (see steps 4-6, pages 28-29).

Pull up cords in the heading tape to the track width and secure. Attach hooks, evenly spaced, across the heading. Knot the nylon cord to the ring at the lower edge of the vertical tape on the opposite side of the blind from the cord lock. Thread cord through the loops to the top. Leave an extra length of cord the width and length of the blind before cutting off. Continuing in the same way, add all the cords.

6 Hang the blind from the track and thread each length of cord through the cord holder above the tape and out to the cord lock at the side. Fix the cleat on the same side of the window as the cord lock. Knot the cords together and wind around the cleat. The blind can then be raised when required.

Austrian blind

Closely woven cotton is suitable for a lined Austrian blind like the one illustrated here, while fine fabrics like lace, muslin or voile are suitable for unlined blinds.

To make the required width, it will often be necessary to join widths of fabric. To avoid an unsightly seam down the centre of the blind, stitch half widths to the side of the central fabric.

Before making the blind, fix a blind track suitable for Austrian or festoon blinds in place at the window (see pages 60-61). Alternatively, mount ordinary curtain track on to a batten (see pages 20-21).

MATERIALS: Furnishing fabric, lining fabric, deep pencil pleat heading tape, blind track, Austrian blind tape and cord, small curtain rings, matching threads, curtain hooks, cleat and screws for fixing

FABRIC: Follow the instructions for measuring the windows and calculating the quantities of fabric and materials required (see pages 62-63)

1 Stitch lengths of fabric together with open seams to make up the required width, ensuring that pattern matches across the joined lengths (see pages 24-25). Join widths of lining in the same way.

2 Turn in a single 5cm (2in) hem down each side and along the lower edge of the top fabric and press. Mitre the corners (see pages 82-83) and use large herringbone stitches to hold.

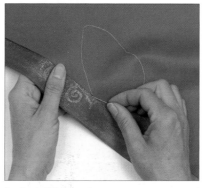

lining, fold under a 1.25cm (½in) hem to the wrong side, then slipstitch lining in place over the side hems. Leave the lower edge free.

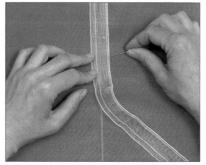

lining up across the blind. Tack tapes in place, then stitch along each side edge. Turn under a 1.25cm (½in) hem on the lining, with the tape ends tucked inside and slipstitch to the top fabric hem.

3 Place the lining right side up over the fabric back with 2.5cm (1in) of fabric showing around each side and on the lower edge. The top edge of the lining should be the width of the heading tape below the top fabric edge. Lockstitch the lining to the fabric at any seams between joined widths (see pages 38-39). On the side edges of the

4 Position a length of tape over the inner edge of each side hem, with raw tape end at the finished edge of the lower hem. Mark vertical lines across the blind at equally spaced intervals of 30-40cm (12-16in). Pin tapes in position, centring over each marked line with loop positions

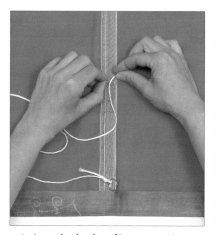

RINGS WITHOUT STITCHES

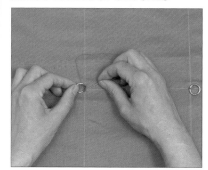

Mark vertical lines as in step 4. Draw in horizontal lines at 15-23cm (6-9in) intervals to within 15cm (6in) of top edge. Hand stitch a ring in place where lines cross and also where lines start at hem edges.

5 Attach the heading tape, (see Applying Heading Tape, pages (28-29). Cut a length of cord and tie it to the bottom ring of tape and thread it vertically up through the loops and out to the side. Repeat for each line of tape. Gather the heading tape to fit the blind track length and secure.

6 Hang the blind, then position the cord holders and thread the cords through the holders and out to one side (see pages 60-61). Fix the cleat below the cord lock and pull the blind cords to ensure that the blind gathers equally across the width. When satisfied, knot the cords together and trim the ends. Pull up the blind and secure around the cleat.

Sewing Techniques

Choosing the right seam to join a particular fabric, creating a hardwearing join, making corners lie flat or knowing how to hand finish correctly are all essential skills if your work is to have a professional finish.

This chapter explains in detail how to create a range of different seams, mitre corners and work the essential hand stitches. It also includes the techniques for stitching piping, adding frills, making borders and applying decorative edgings.

Essential sewing kit

If you already enjoy sewing, most of the items here will be in your workbox. With care, good quality sewing tools will last for years, so if you need to buy new, go for the best you can afford. If you don't have a workbox, buy one or make one, and save yourself hours of searching for tape measure and scissors.

MEASURING AND MARKING

Tape measure: a vital part of any sewing kit. Choose a tape measure made of nylon or some other material that will not stretch and that has metal protective ends. Each side of the tape should start and finish at opposite ends so that you do not have to unwind the tape to find the starting point.

Tailor's chalk: comes in a range of colours but white is easiest to remove later. Keep the edge sharp or alternatively use a chalk pencil which has a brush for removing the marks.

Steel tape: the most reliable tool for measuring items like furniture or windows when working out quantities of material required.

Pencil: for copying patterns on to tracing paper. A soft pencil such as a 2B, is the easiest to use.

CUTTING

Cutting-out scissors: should have a 15cm (6in) blade and be flat on one side. Never use on any other material except fabric.

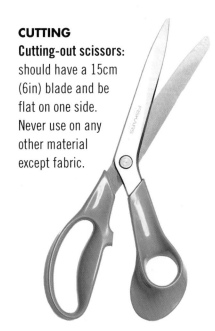

Pinking shears: have a serrated blade which makes a zigzag cut. They are used to neaten raw edges, particularly on fabrics that fray easily.

Needlework scissors: are necessary for snipping threads, cutting into or notching seams, making buttonholes and other close trimming jobs.

STITCHING

Pins: come in a wide range of sizes. Those with glass or plastic heads are the easiest to use. Have a pincushion handy to store unused pins, that way you can avoid finding them later by accident.

Needles: keep a good range of needle types and sizes in your work-box to cover all kinds of fabric and trims. The most useful are:-
Sharps: long needles used for tacking and gathering.
Betweens: small, sharp needles used for hand-sewing.
Ball-point: used on knitted fabrics to prevent snagging.
Bodkins: short, blunt needles used for threading cord and elastic through casings.

MACHINE SEWING

Sewing machines: available in a wide range of different models and are a worthwhile investment that should last a lifetime. Almost all models do a basic lockstitch and a zigzag stitch for neatening edges which is all that is needed to complete the projects in this book.

Machine needles: always select needles to match your fabric – from number 70 for fine fabrics to 110 for thicker ones.

PRESSING

You'll need a good, clean, dry and steam iron, plus a clean ironing board. Keep a clean cloth for pressing delicate fabrics and for when you need extra steam on hard-to-press creases in natural fabrics.

THE RIGHT THREAD FOR THE JOB

Cotton: smooth, strong thread with a slight sheen. Use this on cotton fabric.

Mercerised cotton thread: all-purpose thread, suitable for a variety of fabrics.

Cotton-wrapped polyester: the polyester provides strength while the cotton provides smoothness and lustre.

Silk thread: use for stitching silk and hand-tacking fine fabrics (as it leaves no marks).

Tacking thread: loosely twisted cotton thread, easy to break and so quick to remove from fabric.

Buttonhole twist: use for topstitching as well as buttonholes. Available in synthetic or silk.

Hand stitches

Hand stitches are necessary for specific stages in the making up process and are essential for creating a professional finish. The stitches illustrated here are needed to make the projects in this book.

LOCKSTITCH

1 Lay fabrics together with wrong sides facing. Pin together on the centre line, vertically down the length of the fabrics. Fold back the lining to the pinned line.

Starting about 30cm (12in) from the lower edge secure the thread in the lining with a knot. Make a tiny stitch in the main fabric, picking up just one thread. Leave a 2.5cm (1in) gap, then make a one-thread stitch from the lining back to the top fabric, working over the thread to form a simple loop.

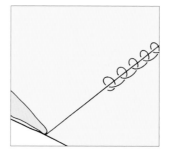

2 Continue making locking stitches every 2.5cm (1in) until you reach the top edge. Keep the thread very loose to ensure that the fabric does not pucker.

Unfold the fabric before smoothing the layers back together. Make another vertical row of pins 38cm (15in) from the last. Fold back the lining, continue making rows of stitches across the complete width of the fabrics until the layers are joined and they act as one.

LADDER STITCH

This is the method used to tack two pieces of a patterned fabric together so that the pattern matches exactly across the seam. Once complete turn the fabric to the wrong side to stitch.

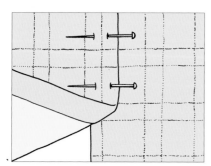

1 On the edge of one of the two pieces of fabric to be joined, press under 1.25cm (½in). Place the folded edge, over the second piece, matching the raw edges and the pattern. Pin in position.

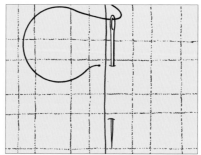

2 Fix the thread within the fold line, make a small stitch across to the other piece of fabric. Following the fold make a long stitch on the underside of the fabric 1.5-2cm (½-¾in) in length.

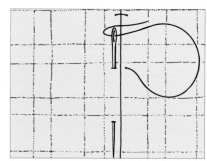

3 Take the needle straight across to the folded side of the fabric, make another long stitch inside the folded edge for another 1.5-2cm (½-¾in). Repeat for the length of the seam.

HERRINGBONE STITCH

This is the stitch used to hold interlinings in place but it can also be used to fix a raw-edged hem.

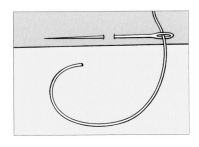

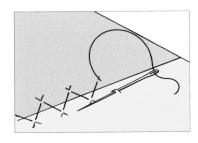

1 Tack the interlining in place to the fabric it is to back. Secure the thread under the interlining and bring the needle up through it, then working from left to right, take the thread diagonally to the main fabric and take a small back stitch of one to two threads only in the main fabric.

2 Still working diagonally, move across to the interlining and make another small back stitch through the interlining only. Continue in this way to the end and secure the thread in the interlining.

SLIPSTITCHING SEAMS

This is used to join two folded edges together and is used when a gap is left in stitching to turn an item through from the wrong to the right side.

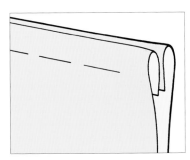

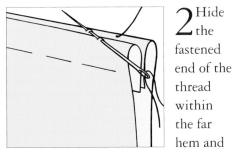

1 Fold under a narrow hem on both pieces of fabric to be joined. Tack to hold folded edges together.

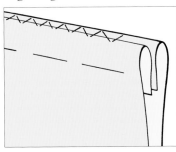

2 Hide the fastened end of the thread within the far hem and then, with folded edges held together, bring the thread into the inner side of the fold of the near hem and take a small stitch. Then take a second small stitch further along in the far hem and pull the thread.

3 Continue in this way until the opening is closed. Do not pull the thread too tight and ensure that stitches and thread are as invisible as possible.

SLIPSTITCHING HEMS

Although machine stitching a hem is quicker, slipstitching creates a neater finish as the stitches are almost invisible on the right side of the fabric.

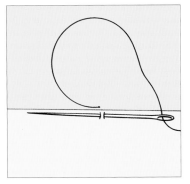

1 Fasten the thread with a knot or backstitch in the fabric of the hem and then bring the needle out on the folded edge of the hem. Pick up one thread, or at the most two, from the main fabric close to the hem edge.

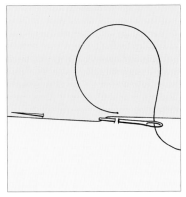

2 Take a long stitch of 2-2.5cm (¾-1in) along the fold of the hem and pull the thread through. Continue in this way, picking up a thread from the main fabric and taking a long stitch, along the hem edge until the hem is stitched.

Seams and hems

Machine stitched seams and hems are tough and hard-wearing. There are several types of seam from which to choose, ranging from a simple open seam to enclosed seams like a flat fell or French seam.

ZIGZAG STITCH

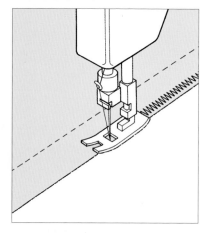

A machine zigzag stitch is commonly used to neaten the raw edge of the seam allowance on open seams where the seam will not be covered. Set the machine for a short and narrow zigzag and stitch down the allowance, slightly in from the edge. Trim the edge just short of the stitches. On fabrics that fray badly use a wider stitch.

TOPSTITCHED HEM

A topstitched hem, worked on a machine, provides a strong result in the minimum of time. However, it is much more obvious than a hand-stitched hem.

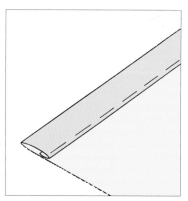

1 Press under a single narrow hem to the wrong side. Then turn the hem to the required width, forming a double hem. Tack in position.

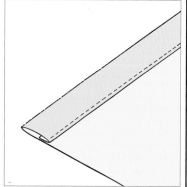

2 Working from the wrong side of the fabric, machine stitch the hem close to the inner folded edge.

OPEN SEAM

This is the seam most commonly used to stitch two lengths of fabric together and is used for all main seams on curtains and blinds where the raw edge will be covered by a lining.

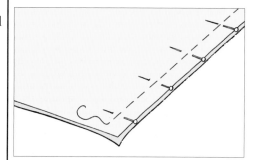

1 With right sides facing, pin the two pieces of fabric together 1.25cm (½in) from the raw edges. Tack just inside the seamline if tacking is considered necessary.

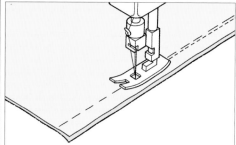

2 Set the machine to reverse, starting 1.25cm (½in) from the end, stitch back to the start on the seamline. Then stitch forwards removing any pins as you work and finish by reverse stitching.

FLAT FELL SEAM

The raw edge of a flat fell seam is encased within the seam but, unlike a French seam, both lines of stitching appear on the surface. This makes it a very tough seam which is ideal for use on furnishings like bedding or table linen that are regularly laundered. Here the stitching is done on the back of the fabric but it can also be done on the front.

FRENCH SEAMS

A French seam is really two seams, one enclosed within the other. The raw edges are contained within the finished seam giving a tough fray-free finish on the wrong side. It is a neat, narrow seam that is ideal for use on sheer fabrics.

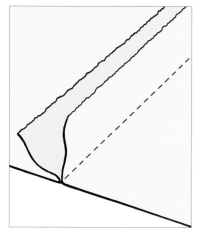

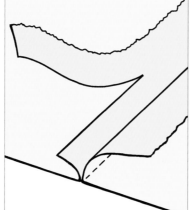

1 With right sides together match up the raw edges of the fabric pieces. Pin, tack and then stitch 1.25cm (½in) from the raw edge.

2 Press to one side. Then trim the seam allowance on the underside of the seam to just under 5mm (¼in).

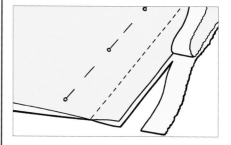

1 With wrong sides together, match raw edges of the pieces of fabric to be joined. Pin, then stitch 5mm (¼in) outside the finished seam line. If necessary, trim close to stitched line.

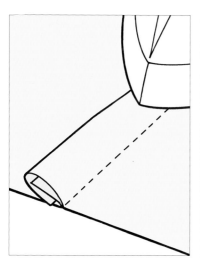

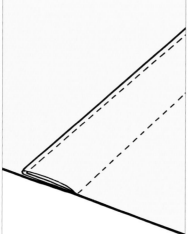

3 Press the wider seam allowance in half with the narrower allowance encased in it. Then press the seam down on to the back of the fabric.

4 Pin the seam in place and tack to hold it secure while you work. Then machine stitch the seam close to the folded edge.

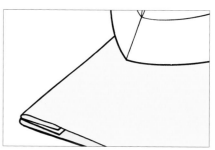

2 Press the seam flat. Turn with right sides of the fabric together and with this first seam line on the edge, press well.

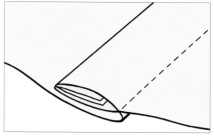

3 Tack, then stitch along the finished seam line. Press.

Corners

Corners need a little extra care, and some special stitching and trimming, if they are to wear well and look good.

Mitring a corner, then cutting away the excess fabric will make it less bulky. A similar effect can be achieved by simply folding the excess fabric into the mitre to create a mock mitre. Folding rather than cutting a mitre is a practical choice if it is likely that the curtain hems will be dropped at a later date.

MOCK MITRE

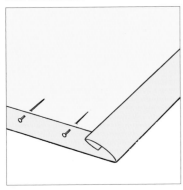

1 A mock mitre is used to reduce bulk on corners without cutting away fabric. Turn in and press double hems along the sides and bottom of the fabric, pin in place.

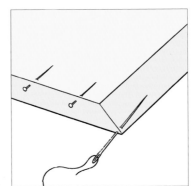

2 Fold in the lower hem at each corner on the diagonal, so that the fold meets the inner side hem edge and looks like a mitre. Slipstitch the corner fold to secure.

STITCHING CORNERS

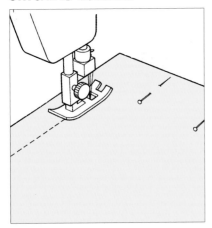

1 To get a sharp angle when stitching a corner, stop one stitch away from the corner and do the last stitch slowly, using the hand wheel if necessary. Leave the needle down in the fabric.

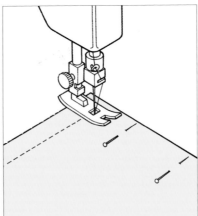

2 Raise the foot and turn the fabric, then lower the foot and continue stitching. To give the corner extra strength use a shorter stitch just before and after the corner.

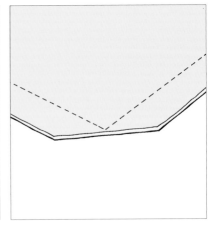

3 Trim the fabric diagonally across the corner just outside the corner point. This ensures that the corner lies flat when turned to the right side.

MITRING AN EVEN HEMMED CORNER

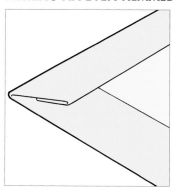

1 On the side and lower edges of the fabric press under a single hem to the wrong side. Then turn under another hem to make a double hem. Press well so that the edge lines of the hems are clear.

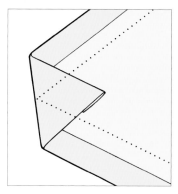

2 Unfold the second part of the hem only. Fold the fabric diagonally, so that the fold runs across the corner point of the finished hem edge. Press this fold, then open out all pressed edges.

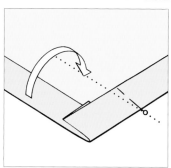

3 With right sides of the fabric facing, fold the fabric at the corner diagonally, with the angled fold lines on top of one another.

Tack 5mm (¼in) outside this fold line to the first hem fold line only.

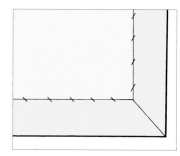

4 Stitch along tacked line, then trim the raw edge to 5mm (¼in), cutting right across the corner. Press seam flat, then turn hem right side out, using a pair of round-ended scissors to push the corner out. Finally, with the hems back in place, slipstitch hems.

MITRING AN UNEVEN HEMMED CORNER

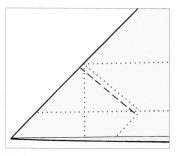

1 Press under a single hem as step 1 above. Press in a double hem on what will be the narrower edge, then mark with a pin where hem edge meets lower pressed hem edge.

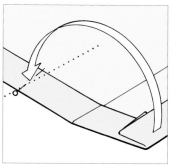

2 Open out and then repeat with the wider hem, marking the point where it meets the narrower hem edge.

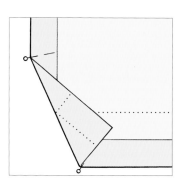

3 Unfold the second part of the hem only and, with single hems in position, press the corner fabric diagonally from one pin mark to the other.

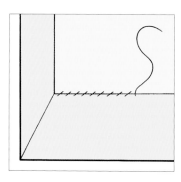

4 Then either trim the corner fabric (see steps 3 and 4 above) or replace the double hems and slipstitch mitred corner without removing corner fabric.

Piping and frills

Piping creates a neat finish to an edge or seam. It can be made with piping cord sandwiched between fabric to form a smooth, rounded edge or without the cord to make flat piping.

Single and double frills are simple to make and can be attached to curtains, blinds and tiebacks to give a more elaborate finish.

PIPING

To work out the fabric requirements, measure all the edges to be piped. Add 5cm (2in) for every join to give the total length of fabric strips and piping required. When buying cotton piping cord allow for shrinkage and wash the cord before using. Fabric which is to be used for piping is cut on the bias.

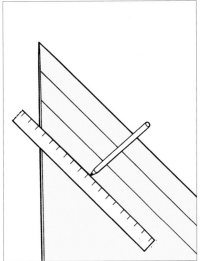

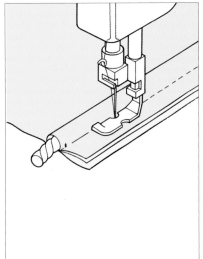

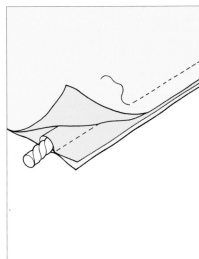

1 Lay fabric flat with the selvages at the sides, remove the selvages. Fold over a top corner diagonally, press. With a dressmakers pencil, draw lines parallel to the fabric fold at 5cm (2in) intervals. Cut the fabric strips. To make a continuous length, pin the fabric together, right sides facing, along the straight grain. Stitch together with narrow seams. Trim the seams and press open.

2 Fold the fabric strip in half lengthways, right side outside, and encase the piping cord inside the strip. Pin, then machine stitch using a zipper foot along the strip close to the cord. Place the stitching line of the piping over the seam line of the fabric, with raw edges matching. Pin, tack, then stitch, starting 1.25cm (½in) from the piping end.

3 Where piping meets, stop stitching 5cm (2in) before the end. Trim cord ends to meet, leaving a 1.25cm (½in) overlap of fabric. Turn the overlap under 6mm (¼in). Wrap around the cord and stitch across the join. Position the second piece of fabric over the piped stitching line with right sides together and raw edges matching. Tack in place along the seam line, stitch, then turn right side out and press.

SINGLE FRILL

The depth of frill depends on the furnishing to which it is to be attached. As a rough guide choose between 6.5-10cm (2½-4in). Then add seam and hem allowances. Measure the length of the edges to which the frill is to be added then double for frill length.

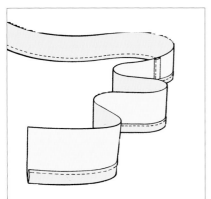

1 Remove the selvages from the fabric. Then, working across the fabric width on the wrong side, mark out with a dressmaker's pencil, strips the width of the frill depth. Cut enough strips to make up the complete frill. Join strips with narrow French seams, (see pages 82-83). On one long edge, turn under then stitch a double 1.25cm (½in) hem to the wrong side. Repeat for short ends and join with a French seam to make a continuous length.

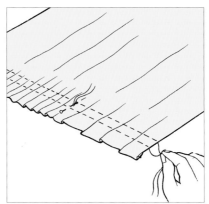

2 Using the longest machine stitch, run two rows of gathering threads along the raw edge. Stitch in lengths of about 60cm (24in). Backstitch at one end to secure and leave a length of thread at the opposite end for pulling up. Gather the frill evenly to fit the fabric edge. To secure the gathers wind the thread ends around pins. With raw edges together and right sides facing tack, then stitch in position. Neaten the raw edges.

DOUBLE FRILL

1 Estimate the length of fabric required for a double frill in the same way as for the single frill but allowing twice the depth plus 2.5cm (1in) for the seam allowance. Join the strips with open seams then fold in half lengthways with the right side inside, stitch the ends to secure. For a continuous frill, join the ends together.

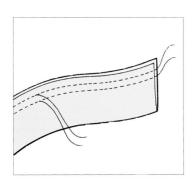

2 Turn the fabric strip right side out, refold and press. Stitch rows of gathering threads through both layers along the raw edge (see Single Frill), pulling up the threads in the same way. Tack the frill to the main fabric with right sides facing and raw edges matching, then stitch in place before neatening the raw edges.

BINDING RAW EDGES

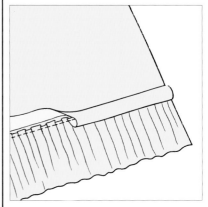

For a neat bound edge allow an extra seam allowance of 3.5cm (1½in) on the main fabric. When the frill has been stitched in place encase the frill raw edge with the wide main fabric edge, tuck under 1.25cm (½in) then slipstitch or machine stitch in place.

Borders

A border acts like a frame, giving the edge of a curtain, blind or valance definition. It can be used to link the window treatment visually with other furnishings in the room and is a clever way of enlarging curtains or blinds for use in a new setting.

A plain border can be made as a complete frame or attached to the sides and the lower edge only. On curtains, a border can be stitched to the leading and lower edges only.

An applied edging strip, cut to the outline of a fabric's motif, adds a decorative finish to the plain edge of a roller blind or a pelmet. Alternatively, use it to co-ordinate a bought blind with the curtains or other furnishings in the room.

APPLIED DECORATIVE BORDER

Choose a fabric with a bold motif that is easy to cut around. You will need a strip of fabric the chosen depth by the width of the edge to which is to be attached. If the border is to be attached to a blind, it will be necessary to make a new pocket for the lath above where the border is to be attached, as the lower edge of an applied border will sit just within the lower edge of a blind, Remove the lath, unstitch the existing casing, then make a new casing (see step 3, pages 66-67). When applying a border to unstiffened fabric, follow the motif outlines with satin stitch once the two fabrics are joined to stop the fabric fraying.

1 Decide on the length and width of the border required, then mark this on the border fabric. Draw around the outline of the motifs on the right side of the fabric using tailor's chalk.

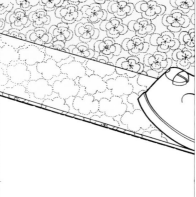

2 Position a strip of double-sided iron-on interfacing, slightly larger than the area to be cut, on the wrong side of the border fabric. Peel off the backing paper and press in place. Cut out the border following the outline.

3 Place the border just inside the pelmet or blind lower edge on the fabric right side, with side edges matching. Press the border in place then trim the lower edge following the border outline.

DOUBLE BORDER

A double border is a piece of folded fabric which is attached to the main fabric at the front and the back, with the raw edges of the main fabric sandwiched between the two halves of the border strip. When using this type of border, no hem allowance is required on the fabric for the curtain or blind.

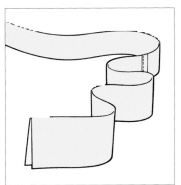

1 First measure each raw edge to which the border is to be attached. Add 2.5cm (1in) for seam allowances to the length measurement of each border piece. Decide on the width of border required, double this measurement and add 2.5cm (1in) for seam allowances. Using these measurements cut out border pieces, join the fabric where necessary to make longer lengths. Cut separate borders for each side.

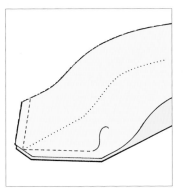

2 Press each border piece in half along its length, right side outside. Where border pieces are to join at right angles, create a diagonal on each piece by folding the raw long edge over to the folded outer edge. Press to mark the diagonal then trim 1.25cm (½in) outside the diagonal fold line, open out. With right sides facing, stitch corners together along the diagonal fold lines. Press, turn right side out then fold into an L-shaped border, press.

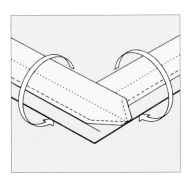

3 Sandwich the main fabric inside the border pieces with raw edge matching border fold and lightly mark the border raw edge line on the right side with tailors chalk. Remove border and mark a further line 1.25cm (½in) outside the first. Replace border lower edge with right sides of fabrics matching. Line up border raw edge to outer draw line with mitre inner corner on any corner points. Stitch lower edge. Repeat for side edges. Turn in any short raw ends and slipstitch closed.

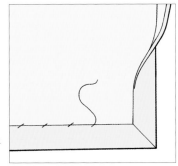

4 Press, then turn the border over the end of the fabric, sandwiching the main fabric between the border. Press under a 1.25cm (½in) seam allowance along the raw edge of the back border and tack in place on the wrong side of the fabric. Slipstitch in place following the stitching line on the front border edge.

USING A BORDER TO INCREASE THE FABRIC SIZE

When a border is used to increase the size of a curtain or a blind, border pieces need to be cut to fit its finished rather than its existing size. Work out the length required for the side border pieces, and add the border depth measurement to the side measurement of the curtain or blind. For the lower border piece, add twice border depth measurement to the lower edge measurement. Attach the border to the main fabric, positioning it with right sides facing and raw edges matching.

Finishing touches

Making neat seams can be very satisfying, but that doesn't mean you always have to leave them visible. Braid, cord and ribbon can all be used to decorate the finished project, and using co-ordinating colours can do much to enhance your colour scheme.

BRAID

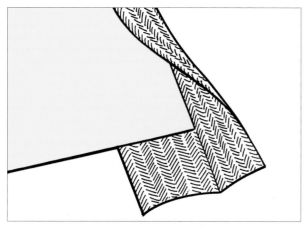

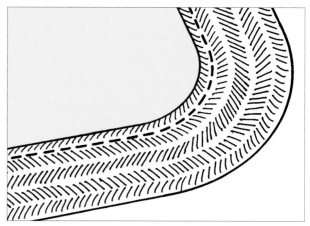

1 Apply fold-over braid with the narrower edge on the fabric's right side, tacking both layers in place through the fabric.

2 Topstitch from the right side close to the edge. This also catches the slightly wider band of braid on the wrong side.

NARROW BRAID

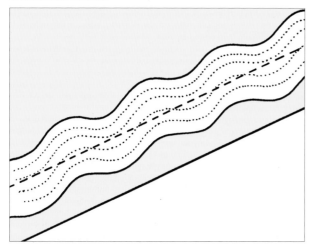

Narrow braid such as ricrac can be attached with a single line of topstitching down the centre.

FRINGE

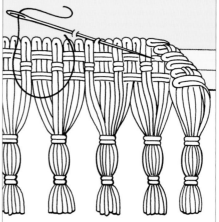

When applying a fringe to the lower edge of the curtains or blinds, begin by turning a narrow hem to the right side of the fabric. Then tack the fringe braid edge in place over this hem and machine stitch in position.

CORD

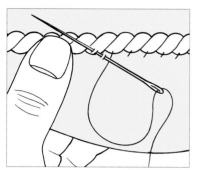

1 If the cord is not to be attached to the edge of the fabric, mark the line it is to follow with tailor's chalk or tacking. Stitch cord in place using slipstitch and a thread that matches the background fabric. Use your other hand to hold the cord in position as you work.

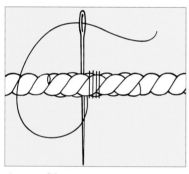

2 To join cord allow 1.25cm (½in) at each end for joining. Trim one end and dot on fabric glue to stop it from fraying. Allow to dry. Trim the other end, apply a dot of glue to this, then press in place to the end of the first length. Allow glue to dry and slipstitch the new length in position. To disguise the join, cover it with a circle of matching threads.

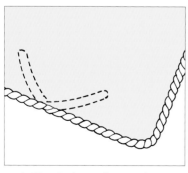

3 If the join meets over a seam, insert both cord ends in the seam. Close the seam and slipstitch cords together on the top edge to form a continuous line.

RIBBON

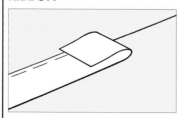

When applying ribbon, first mark where it is to go with tailor's chalk. Tack the ribbon in place over the marked line. When applying satin ribbon, which shows stitch marks, tack close to the edges. To attach the ribbon, topstitch down each side using straight stitch. Alternatively use zigzag or a decorative embroidery stitch over the edges of the ribbon.

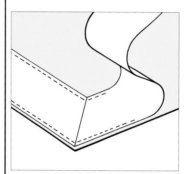

When applying ribbon along the edge of fabric, turn the hem on the fabric to the wrong side to the width of the ribbon. Line up the ribbon with the hem edge, mitring at the corners, machine stitch in place along either side.

CURTAIN FINISHING TIPS

• As heavy curtains may drop when hung, altering the level of the hem, it pays to hang them up for a few days before the hem is finally stitched. Include curtain weights in the hem to ensure that curtains hang well.

• On curtains or blinds, use a cord tidy to contain the pulled-up heading cords neatly at the outside edge of the curtain. Alternatively, wind the cords around your hand to create a neat bundle then tie together with a plastic bag twist closure. Doing this makes it easier to stretch the tape flat before laundering or dry cleaning the curtains or blinds.

• Once hung, draw the curtains back then arrange them in neat folds before loosely tying in place with strips of spare fabric at the top, bottom and centre. Leave for a couple of days to allow the folds to 'set' before removing the ties. In the same way, raise Roman blinds to the top of the window, arrange and press the pleats in place with your hands and leave to 'set' for a few days.

CORDED TIEBACK
Pages 44-45

SCALLOP-EDGED TIEBACK
Page 45

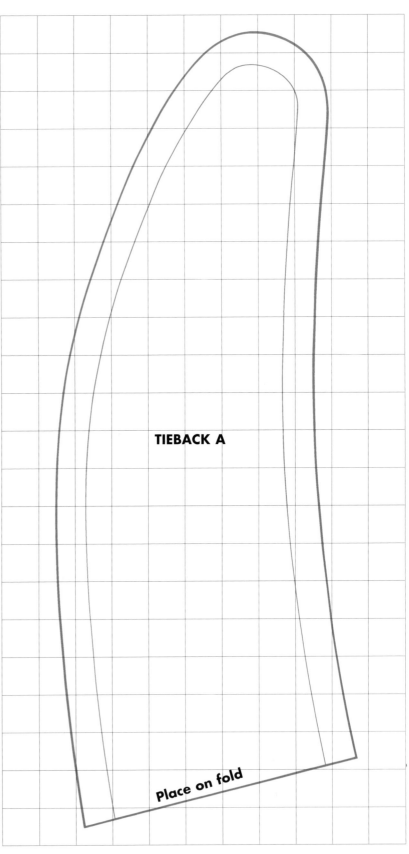

TIEBACK A

Place on fold

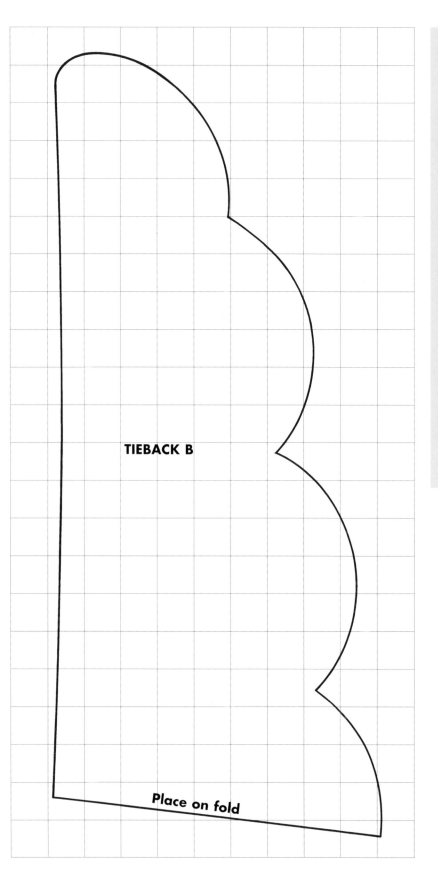

TIEBACK B

Place on fold

SCALING UP

The templates for Tieback A and Tieback B can be enlarged or reduced on a photocopier to make them the required size. Alternatively, the templates can be enlarged by hand. To do this, draw a grid on a piece of paper, increasing the size of the 1cm (½in) squares printed on the templates proportionately to the increase in size that is required. So, if you wish to make a template twice the size, draw a grid with 2cm (¾in) squares. Then, one square at a time, draw in each part of the pattern, reproducing the image in a scaled up version in the larger square.

Glossary

Batten
A length of sawn timber that is placed above a window to take the fixings for a blind or a curtain track.

Bias
A slantwise angle to the straight weft and warp threads of a fabric. Strips cut on the bias are used for piping and binding as they stretch and can be applied around a curve without puckering.

Clipping
Making snips at regular intervals into the seam allowance allows the fabric to stretch and give where necessary when it is turned to the right side.

Double hem
When fabric is folded twice so that the raw edge is hidden within the hem.

Flat fell seam
A very tough seam where the raw edge is encased within the seam and both lines of stitching appear on the surface. Ideal for use on furnishings that are laundered regularly.

Flush window
A window that is level with the surface of the wall on all sides. Curtains and blinds for flush windows are usually made larger than the window size.

French seam
A neat, narrow seam which is really two seams, one enclosed within the other. Ideal for use on sheer fabrics.

Grain
The direction in which the fibres run in a length of fabric.

Interfacing
Special material, available in sew-in or iron-on forms, which is attached to the wrong side of the main fabric to provide stiffness, shape and support.

Interlining
An extra layer of fabric, placed between the main fabric and lining, to add insulation, thickness and weight.

Iron-on
The term used to describe the chemical reaction when one fabric (usually interfacing) is fused to another with a warm iron.

Ladder stitch
The professional method used to tack two pieces of a patterned fabric together so that the pattern matches across the seam.

Lath
A thin strip of wood that is slotted inside a pocket in the fabric of a blind and used to hold the fabric flat along its lower edge.

Mitre
Used on a corner between two right-angled sides, a mitre gives a neat angled join that does away with surplus fabric.

Motif
The dominant element in a fabric design.

Notching
Making V-shaped cuts into the seam allowance to a point just outside the seam. This is used on a very curved seam to ensure that the seam allowance lies flat when the fabric is turned to the right side.

Open seam
The simplest way to join two pieces of fabric together. Fabrics are placed right sides together, machine stitched along a seamline parallel to the fabric raw edge and then pressed open. Used where a lining will cover the seam and hide any raw edges. Also known as a flat seam.

Pattern repeat
The depth of one complete design in a length of fabric, which is then repeated along the cloth.

Pelmet shelf
A narrow shelf with a front edge from which a pelmet hangs. The width of the shelf keeps the pelmet fabric away from the curtains or blind behind and stops the two from becoming tangled.

Recessed window
A window that is set back from the wall surface. Curtains or blinds can either be made to fit inside the recess or fixed to the wall surface.

Seam allowance
The area between the seamline and the raw edge. The seam allowance needs to be neatened, especially on fabric that frays easily.

Seam line
The line designated for stitching the seam.

Selvage
A plain, narrow strip down either side that stops uncut fabric from fraying. The selvage should be removed before the fabric is cut out.

Single hem
When fabric is folded once, either to the front or back, so that the raw edge is exposed. A single hem is usually used when the hem will be covered by another piece of fabric.

Slipstitch
An almost invisible stitch used for securing hems or joining two folded edges on the right side of the fabric.

Straight grain
This follows the warp threads, which run down the length of the fabric parallel to the selvages.

Tacking
A temporary stitch to hold fabrics in position and act as a guide for permanent stitching.

Tension
The balance and tightness of the needle and bobbin threads on a sewing machine that combine to create the perfect stitch.

Topstitch
A line of stitching on the right side of the fabric, often used as a decorative highlight.

Warp
Parallel threads running lengthways down woven fabric, interlacing with the weft threads.

Weft
Threads that run from side to side across woven fabric, interlacing with the warp threads.

Index

Curtains and Blinds

Credits and acknowledgements.

*The author and publishers would like to thank the following for
their assistance in producing this book:*

With special thanks to Myra Bowden and Ronda Purkess for stitchwork and also
to Sarah Newman. For the generous provision of fabric, accessories and props, Anna French,
London SW3: pages 44, 52, 66, 70. Castle Gardens, Sherborne, Dorset. Crowson Fabrics Ltd,
Uckfield, East Sussex: pages 28, 30, 34, 38, 46, 49, 50, 68, 72. Cope and Timmins, London
N18. Charles and Dickens, Yeovil, Somerset. Laura Ashley London: 36, 48, 54.
Malabar, London SW8: page 40. Rufflette Limited, Wythenshawe, Manchester.
Walter Wall Carpets, Yeovil, Somerset.

Picture Credits
Elizabeth Whiting & Associates: All pictures on pages 4-5, 6, 7, 16, 17, 22 and 59

Written by:	Jenny Plucknett	
Project editor:	Finny Fox-Davies	
Editor:	Laura Potts	
Art director:	Graham Webb	
Designers:	Design Section	
Photography:	George Wright	
Picture research:	Nell Hunter	
Illustrator:	Geoff Denny Associates	
Production controller:	Louise McIntyre	

Jenny Plucknett has asserted her right to be
identified as the author of this work

First published 1998

© Haynes Publishing 1998

Published by Haynes Publishing
Sparkford, Nr Yeovil, Somerset BA22 7JJ

British Library Cataloguing-in-Publication Data:
A catalogue record of this book is available from
the British Library

ISBN 1 85960 318 1

Printed in France by
Imprimerie Pollina S.A.